The Limits of Lockean Rights in Property

THE LIMITS OF LOCKEAN RIGHTS IN PROPERTY

Gopal Sreenivasan

New York   Oxford
OXFORD UNIVERSITY PRESS
1995

Oxford University Press

Oxford New York
Athens Auckland Bangkok Bombay
Calcutta Cape Town Dar es Salaam Delhi
Florence Hong Kong Istanbul Karachi
Kuala Lumpur Madras Madrid Melbourne
Mexico City Nairobi Paris Singapore
Taipei Tokyo Toronto

and associated companies in
Berlin Ibadan

Copyright © 1995 by Gopal Sreenivasan

Published by Oxford University Press, Inc.
198 Madison Avenue, New York, New York 10016

Oxford is a registered trademark of Oxford University Press

All rights reserved. No part of this publication may be reproduced,
stored in a retrieval system, or transmitted, in any form or by any means,
electronic, mechanical, photocopying, recording, or otherwise,
without the prior permission of Oxford University Press.

Library of Congress Cataloging-in-Publication Data
Sreenivasan, Gopal.
The limits of lockean rights in property / Gopal Sreenivasan.
p. cm.
Includes bibliographical references and index.
ISBN 0-19-509176-0
1. Locke, John, 1632–1704. Two treatises of government.
2. Locke, John, 1632–1704—Views on property. 3. Locke, John,
1632–1704—Contributions in political science. 4. Property.
I. Title.
JC153.L87S68 1995
320.1'01—dc20   94-32889

9 8 7 6 5 4 3 2 1
Printed in the United States of America
on acid-free paper

To my Amma and Appa

Preface

This little book descends, largely by addition, from the B.Phil. thesis I submitted in Oxford in Trinity Term, 1988. A considerable part of the delay in its reaching this stage is due to the infrequency with which I was able to make time to work on it while completing a Ph.D. in Berkeley. In the interval, of course, a prodigious amount of work on Locke and his account of property has appeared in print, so that I sometimes have had the feeling *devant moi le déluge*. I have tried, by and large, to respond to this work in the course of my discussion, certainly to the extent that it presents some clear argument for a thesis either contrary or complementary to one of my own. I regret, however, that John Simmons's recent book *The Lockean Theory of Rights* has reached me too late to discuss here. But I take some encouragement from the fact that we are in agreement on a number of points, at least in the form of our conclusions.

In the course of preparing this work, I have profited from the assistance of a number of teachers and friends. My greatest debt is to my B.Phil. supervisor, Jerry Cohen, and I am pleased to have a forum more public than an obscure corner of Duke Humphrey's Library in which to thank him. It was he who originally encouraged me to publish the thesis, and his unfailingly generous, rigorous, and instructive supervision accounts for so much of it surviving in the present discussion. He was furthermore kind enough to continue to read and criticise new material, even after I had left Oxford. Christopher Taylor, who chaired the examination committee in my year, helpfully allowed me to read the notes he had made, and I should like to thank him, as well as Daniel Bell and David Keen, for various useful comments on the thesis. I am extremely grateful to James Tully for his invaluable encouragement, support, and advice, as I am to Samuel Scheffler, who took a supererogatory interest in a project that had nothing to do with my dissertation and not only made helpful comments about the whole manuscript, but very kindly encouraged me to persevere in face of various obstacles.

Later versions of the manuscript benefited from the criticism of anonymous referees. Thanks also go to the staff at Oxford University Press for all their help. Finally, I should like to thank the Social Sciences and Humanities Research Council of Canada and the Committee of Vice-Chancellors and Principals of the Universities of the United Kingdom for fellowship support of the original thesis, and the University of California, Berkeley, for a Humanities Graduate Research Grant that helped to finance the completion of the project.

Princeton, New Jersey G. S.
June 1994

Contents

1. **Introduction, 3**

    Locke's Property and Lockean Property, 4
    Rights in Property, 7
    The Context of Locke's Argument, 13
    The Consent Problem, 15
    Rights and the Means of Preservation, 17
    Overview, 18

Part I. Property in the *Two Treatises*

2. **Property without Consent, 21**

    Natural Law and Natural Rights, 21
    The Consent Problem, 24
    The Bare Structure, 32
    Money and Scarcity, 35
    Waldron's Critique, 37
    Rights and the Means of Preservation, 41
    Enough and as Good, 47
    Tully and Community Ownership, 50
    Labour's Abundance, 54

3. **Mixing or Making? 59**

    Labour, Mixing, and the Tradition, 60
    The Workmanship Model, 62
    God and Creation, 69
    Man as Maker, 74

Some Objections, 81
A Difficulty, 85
An Asymmetry, 88
The Preservation of Property, 90

Part II. Limitations of Lockean Property

4. Limitations of the Original Theory, 95
Limits in Locke, 96
The Nature of Locke's Property, 96
Conditions of Locke's Property, 100
Charity, 102
Inheritance, 104
Limits to Locke, 106
The Limits of Transmission, 106
Access versus Appropriation, 111
Taking Sufficiency Seriously, 113
The Generation Problem, 118

5. A Latter-Day Lockean, 120
Nozick on Property, 121
The Indeterminacy Objection, 126
Compensation and Comparison, 130
Beyond Productive Bounty, 135

6. Conclusion, 140
The Interpretation of the Argument, 140
The Argument for the Interpretation, 144
The Limits of Lockean Logic, 148

Bibliography, 153

Index, 157

The Limits of Lockean Rights in Property

So long as an educated minority, living off all previous generations, hardly guessed why life was so easy to live, so long as the majority, working day and night, did not quite realize why they received none of the fruits of their labour, both parties believed this to be the natural order of things, and the world of cannibalism could survive. People often take prejudice or habit for truth and in that case feel no discomfort: but if they once realize that their truth is nonsense, the game is up. From then onwards it is only by force that a man can be compelled to do what he considers to be absurd.

Alexander Herzen, *From the Other Shore*

1

Introduction

Though its initial reception was less than encouraging, John Locke's theory of property was soon regarded as one of the foremost treatments of the subject. Its influence in the eighteenth century, both philosophical and practical, was profound and far-reaching, and by the early twentieth century Hastings Rashdall was able to observe that Locke's theory had 'become the basis of almost all the attempts of modern philosophers to base the justification of private property upon some *a priori* principle, and not upon the ground of general utility and convenience.'[1] To judge by the recent literature, contemporary interest in Locke's argument for the legitimacy of private property remains as high as ever. In part, this interest is historical, but Locke's theory also continues to function as a central point of reference for ongoing examinations of the legitimacy of the institution of private property.

In this book, I propose to examine Locke's theory of property from both of these points of view. Although I shall devote considerable attention to the interpretation of the argument that Locke advances for the legitimacy of private property in his *Two Treatises of Government*,[2] my ultimate interest lies in determining what kind of private property right can actually be established on the basis of this argument. This examination leads to a somewhat surprising pair of conclusions: Locke's argument has contemporary relevance and a defensible regime of private

---

1. H. Rashdall, 'The Philosophical Theory of Property,' *Property: Its Duties and Rights*, ed. C. Gore (London: Macmillan, 1913), p. 40.
2. J. Locke, *Two Treatises of Government*, rev. ed., ed. P. Laslett (Cambridge: Cambridge University Press, 1963). All references to this work are by treatise number and section number. Quotations do not retain the italicisation of Laslett's text.

property rights is egalitarian. It is not the individual conclusions that are surprising, of course, but rather their combination and, in particular, the fact that—as we shall discover—the latter conclusion can be demonstrated by means of the former.

Generally speaking, proponents of the contemporary relevance of Locke's argument have also defended the legitimacy of inegalitarian regimes of private property. Indeed, their defence has often been rested precisely on the contemporary relevance of this argument.[3] Proponents of more egalitarian regimes of private property, however, have been apt to criticise the cogency of Locke's argument and so to impugn at least its constructive relevance to contemporary discussion.[4] The relevance of Locke's argument has also been challenged from an altogether different angle, namely, on the ground that his argument has ineluctable theological commitments and hence is powerless to persuade in a secular world.[5]

At least in part, I arrive at this unfamiliar combination of conclusions as a result of the distinction that I enforce between the focus of my *interpretative* interest in Locke's theory of property and the focus of my *evaluative* interest in that same theory. It will, perhaps, help avert confusion in what follows if I articulate this difference clearly at the outset.

Locke's Property and Lockean Property

Insofar as we are concerned with *interpreting* Locke's theory of property, the focus of our interest is the very theory held by the historical figure John Locke. This much is fairly straightforward. Insofar, however, as we are concerned with *evaluating* Locke's theory, the focus of our interest is rather broader. Naturally, our interest here includes, indeed begins with, the very theory held by the historical Locke, but it is not confined to *that* theory. For when it comes to evaluation, the primary focus

---

3. The most prominent example of this is R. Nozick, *Anarchy, State, and Utopia* (Oxford: Basil Blackwell, 1974). Nozick's book will hereinafter be abbreviated *ASU*.
4. A leading example is J. Waldron, *The Right to Private Property* (Oxford: Clarendon Press, 1988). Waldron's book will hereinafter be abbreviated *RPP*.
5. The most forceful statement of this position is J. Dunn, *The Political Thought of John Locke* (Cambridge: Cambridge University Press, 1969).

of our concern is a theory-*type*, as opposed to any particular instance of that type. What we should like to determine is the power of a certain type of argument to legitimate the institution of private property.

Of course, if the very theory held by the historical Locke were an ideal instance of its type, then this distinction between type and instance would be otiose. But that, as we shall see, is not the case. We can identify two main respects in which Locke's own theory is ill qualified as an ideal instance. To begin with, it is ill qualified because it does not consistently adhere to the logic of its own argument. Consequently, Locke's own conclusions do not reflect the true power of his argument to legitimate private property. Assessing the true power of this argument, then, requires us to criticise (and so to move beyond) the theory held by the historical Locke.

Locke's own theory is furthermore ill qualified as an ideal because it incorporates elements which, though consistent with the logic of his argument, are extraneous to it. This is not an argumentative failing of the theory, but it does serve to obscure the fact that one can omit various of Locke's own premises without vitiating the logic of his argument. This is an important fact to recognise, since upholding *these* premises will not be a necessary condition of a theory's being type-identical with Locke's own,[6] and hence these premises fall outside the scope of our evaluative interest in Locke's theory.

We shall maintain that Locke's theory of property has two characteristic elements. The first element consists in a need to divorce the legitimacy of appropriation from the requirement that everyone consent to it, together with an ingenious device for doing so—the stipulation that appropriation not impair anyone's access to the materials needed to produce her subsistence. We shall call this element the *apparatus of the consent problem*. The second element is the principle that individuals are entitled to a property in the products of their making, provided that there is no legitimate objection to their use of the relevant materials. We shall call this element the *doctrine of maker's right*. The conjunction of these elements defines the distinctive logic of Locke's argument.

---

6. The necessary and sufficient condition of a theory's being type-identical with Locke's is that it share the logic of his argument.

Clearly, the identification of what is characteristic in Locke's (or any other) argument can be controversial. Thus, it has been suggested that (virtually) the entire natural law framework of Locke's argument is characteristic of it, thereby entailing that no theory which excludes that framework properly qualifies as Lockean.[7] But despite the importance of natural law to Locke's argument, we cannot suppose that it is *characteristic* of that argument, since (among other reasons) Locke's theory shares this framework with a variety of other theories of property whose argumentative structures differ sharply from its own.[8]

Still, there is no general way of defending the above analysis apart from a detailed consideration of Locke's theory and texts; this we shall undertake in chapters 2 and 3. We anticipate the conclusion of these chapters here simply in order to give some content to the theory-*type* of which the theory held by the historical Locke is, so we submit, the canonical—but not an ideal—instance.

Since the distinction between the interpretative and the evaluative foci of our interest in Locke's theory may otherwise prove difficult to keep in mind, let us introduce the following terminological convention: we shall reserve the possessive *Locke's* to refer to the very theory of property held by the historical Locke and to points related thereto—thus, Locke's theory, Locke's conclusion, and Locke's landowner. We shall reserve the adjective *Lockean* to refer to the type of theory of property that is characterised by the conjunction of the apparatus of the consent problem with the doctrine of maker's right and to points related thereto—thus, a Lockean theory, a Lockean conclusion, and a Lockean landowner.

With the assistance of this convention, we can now perhaps dampen some of the surprise attending our general conclusions. Despite the fact that Locke himself made a fundamental appeal to theological premises, the adoption of a secular outlook does not in the least diminish the contemporary relevance of the Lockean argument for private property. As it happens, neither of the characteristic elements of Locke's argument

---

7. See, e.g., V. Held, 'John Locke on Robert Nozick,' *Social Research* 43 (1976), pp. 269–92.

8. To take but two examples, Locke differs sharply from both Grotius and Tyrrell in his handling of the consent problem, yet their theories both belong to the natural law tradition.

requires a belief in God's existence. The doctrine of maker's right requires no such belief even in Locke's hands, and the apparatus of the consent problem can be reconstructed with functionally equivalent secular premises.

Similarly, the fact that Locke does not consistently adhere to the logic of his own argument is no reason to question the cogency of the Lockean theory of property. This would be to dismiss the substance of Locke's argument simply because of difficulties with his presentation of it. As we shall argue, however, the substance of this argument—in particular, of the logic of the Lockean solution to the consent problem—has the effect of making a regime of Lockean property substantially egalitarian. The legitimacy of Lockean property requires that everyone's access to the means of production be maintained in a manner that conserves her liberty to produce a surplus.

The egalitarianism of the Lockean theory of property is not, of course, without its problems. Foremost among these is the problem of how equality is to be maintained over time. But this is a difficulty that all forms of egalitarianism must confront.[9] What our investigation seeks to establish is that, however attractive, the relevance of the Lockean theory of property to contemporary discussions of distributive justice is as a form of egalitarianism. If this is correct, then defenders of inegalitarian distributions of property may draw support from the Lockean theory only to the extent that they follow Locke in failing to adhere to the logic of its argument.

Rights in Property

In order to examine properly either the nature or the success of an argument for private property, whether it be Locke's or some other, it is essential to have some understanding of just what private property is. Ideally, of course, we should like to have as complete an understanding of the matter as possible, but the question of how private property is exactly to

---

9. See, e.g., R. Dworkin, 'What is Equality? Part 2: Equality of Resources,' *Philosophy and Public Affairs* 10 (4) (1981), pp. 283–345.

be defined is rather intractable.[10] Past a certain point, moreover, further consideration of its intricacies contributes little to one's ability to examine arguments for the legitimacy of the institution. Our aim here, then, will be to present the rudiments of a satisfactory understanding of private property.

Since *private* property represents but one form of property regime, we can begin by distinguishing it from other varieties of property. The challenge is to characterise the notion of a property right quite generally. Having done so, private property is fairly straightforwardly distinguished as the property regime in which this right is primarily vested in private individuals or firms. Robert Nozick's characterisation constitutes a useful starting-point:

> The central core of the notion of a property right in X, relative to which other parts of the notion are to be explained, is the right to determine what shall be done with X; the right to choose which of the constrained set of options concerning X shall be realized or attempted. (*ASU*, p. 171)

On this suggestion, private property in something obtains if a private individual has the right to determine what is to be done with the thing.

One merit of Nozick's characterisation is that it exhibits very clearly the indeterminacy of the general notion of a property right. This notion is indeterminate because, to employ the terms of his analysis, the constrained set of options concerning X—among which the property-holder has the right to choose—remains unspecified. Failing a specification of this constrained set of options, we will be unable to say with any degree of precision what it is that a property right in X entitles the right-holder to do with X. Plainly, this situation can be remedied: given a constrained set of options, a precise determination can be made of the specific rights[11] in X that are conveyed by a property right in X.

In principle, there are any number of constrained sets of options that could be employed to provide the notion of a property right with deter-

---

10. For a helpful general discussion of this question, see Waldron, *RPP*, ch. 2.
11. 'Rights' is used here in the loose sense that was the subject of Hohfeld's analysis. In particular instances, we shall revert to the strict terminology of (claim) rights, liberties (Hohfeld's permissions), powers, and immunities, as appropriate. For the relevant distinctions, see W. N. Hohfeld, *Fundamental Legal Conceptions* (New Haven: Yale University Press, 1919).

minate content. In practice, however, at least as far as regimes of private property have been concerned, the actual variation in the content of a property right across different societies has been limited.[12] Accordingly, it is possible to identify a relatively stable common cluster among the specific rights conferred on property-holders in these regimes.

The classic account of the common features of property in these regimes is found in A. M. Honoré's essay 'Ownership,' which we shall follow here.[13] But before we do so, a number of clarifications are in order. Since Honoré's analysis is restricted to regimes of private property, the determinate features—or *incidents*, as he calls them—of property which he discusses are not to be taken as common to regimes of property generally; rather, his is an account of the standard incidents of liberal (i.e., individual) ownership.

Honoré's analysis is further restricted to the incidents of full, individual ownership in ordinary, uncomplicated cases. He thus abstracts from the complications introduced by split ownership, that is, by cases in which it is controversial whether a thing has a single owner. A thing's having a single owner is consistent, of course, with someone else's having a lesser interest in that thing, but Honoré's discussion does not extend to an account of the various lesser interests which can be held in a thing. Instead he concentrates on the incidents which inhere in 'the person who has the greatest interest in a thing admitted by a mature legal system' (p. 161). Finally, although Honoré does not do so,[14] we shall forgo a discussion of the kinds of things that are capable of being owned in the full liberal sense.

Full individual ownership, on Honoré's account, comprises eleven standard incidents (pp. 166–79), enumerated here with brief explanations where helpful.

---

12. A. M. Honoré, 'Ownership,' in *Making Law Bind* (Oxford: Clarendon Press, 1987), p. 162: 'In [mature legal systems] certain important legal incidents are common to different systems. . . . Ownership, *dominium*, *propriété*, *Eigentum*, and similar words stand not merely for the greatest interest in things in particular systems but for a type of interest with common features transcending particular systems.'

13. Unless otherwise indicated, subsequent internal page cites in this section refer to this essay.

14. See Honoré, 'Ownership,' pp. 179–84; cf. Waldron, *RPP*, pp. 33–37.

1. 'The right to possess'—the right to have exclusive physical control of the thing, so far as its nature admits.
2. 'The right to use'—the liberty of using the thing at one's discretion.
3. 'The right to manage'—the right to decide how and by whom the thing shall be used; this depends chiefly on powers to license acts which would otherwise be unlawful and powers to make contracts.
4. 'The right to the income.'
5. 'The right to the capital'—the power to alienate the thing and the liberty to consume, waste, or destroy the whole part of it.
6. 'The right to security'—an immunity from expropriation, except in certain circumstances.
7. 'The incident of transmissibility'—the heritability of the interest in the thing ad infinitum.
8. 'The incident of absence of term'—the absence of a term beyond which the interest in the thing is due to expire.
9. 'The duty to prevent harm'—the duty not to use the thing harmfully, nor to allow others to do so.
10. 'Liability to execution'—the liability to forfeit the interest in the thing by execution for a judgement debt or on insolvency.
11. 'Residuary character'—the right to the reversion, either immediately or ultimately, of the 'rights' comprised by lesser interests in the thing upon the extinction of those interests.

Now the thorny aspect of the question of how private property is exactly to be defined, or indeed of whether it can be, centres on the issue of what the relation is between the general notion of a private property right (one formulation of which we gave above) and the possible range of specific rights in terms of which a private property right can be made determinate. A special case of this issue is presented by the relation between this same general notion and the standard incidents of liberal ownership enumerated above.

There are two points concerning this relation that bear on an attempt to argue for the legitimacy of private property. For reasons that will become apparent, we shall consider these points with reference to the special case of liberal ownership. The first point is that the standard incidents do not constitute either necessary or sufficient conditions of having private property in something. That is to say, for each of the standard incidents,[15] it is not the case that having that right in X is either necessary or sufficient for owning X. Without entering into a full demonstration of this, it may nevertheless be instructive to consider a few examples.[16] Thus, incident (1) is neither necessary nor sufficient for ownership, since a lessee has the right to possess the thing, but the lessor owns it; the same is true of (3) and (4), since a usufructuary has the right to manage and to take the income of the thing, but the reversioner owns it; the same is also true of (5), since the donee of a power of appointment over trust property has the right to dispose of the capital subject to the power, but the trustee owns the thing.

The conclusion that none of the standard incidents is a necessary condition of liberal ownership can, in fact, be generalised at both ends, to the effect that no specific right is a necessary condition of private property as such.[17] What licenses the generalisation at the front end—to the effect that *no specific right* is a necessary condition of liberal ownership— is the fact that the standard incidents, at least when taken all together, do constitute a set of jointly sufficient conditions of liberal ownership.[18] What licenses it at the back end—to the effect that none of the standard incidents is a necessary condition of *private property as such*—is the fact that liberal ownership is undeniably a form of private property. The sig-

---

15. We should note that incidents (9) and (10) are not rights, even in a loose sense, but rather social limitations on ownership. Hence, unlike the other incidents, they are really not even candidates for the status denied to the standard incidents in the text.

16. Examples are drawn from Honoré, 'Ownership,' pp. 176–79; examples for the other incidents are also to be found there.

17. Honoré holds that the standard incidents are (jointly) necessary elements of ownership in the following sense: 'If a system did not admit them, and did not provide for them to be united in a single person, we would conclude that it did not know the liberal concept of ownership, thought it might have a modified version of ownership, either primitive or sophisticated.' 'Ownership,' p. 165. This is nevertheless consistent with the generalised conclusion for which we shall argue in the text, since liberal ownership is but one form of ownership (i.e., of private property), as Honoré himself recognises.

18. It remains an open question, one that Honoré does not address, whether any subset(s) of this set also constitute jointly sufficient conditions of ownership and, if so, what they are.

nificance of the general conclusion in the present context is this: if no specific right is a necessary condition of private property as such, then the legitimacy of private property as such does *not* entail, for any given specific right, that the inherence of that right is itself legitimate.

This leads us to the second point, which is that arguments for the legitimacy of private property cannot simply dispense with a consideration of which specific rights are themselves legitimate. For instance, Jeremy Waldron suggests that in political philosophy, interest in the legitimacy of private property is confined to the legitimacy of a certain *type* of institution, namely, that given by the general notion of a private property right. As the basis of his suggestion, Waldron adverts to the fact that philosophers are 'not interested (at least in the first instance) in the detail of the property rules of any society in particular' (*RPP*, p. 60).

But we should not conclude from this that philosophers are not interested in the legitimacy of any particular private property regime, that is, in the legitimacy of any specific rights in property. For even if private property as such were shown to be legitimate, it might nevertheless remain the case that no particular determinate private property right was legitimate. This conjuncture could arise if no specific rights in property were themselves legitimate; in light of the first point made above, this is a possibility that cannot be discounted. What we should conclude from Waldron's fact, then, is only that philosophers are interested (in the first instance) in the legitimacy of some or other regime of private property, rather than in the legitimacy of some one regime of private property in particular.

Our examination of Locke's theory of property will abstract from the issue of just what relation holds between the general notion of a private property right and the various specific rights in terms of which that right can be made determinate; in so doing, we shall leave unresolved the apparent ambiguity of the expression 'private property.' For the most part, our discussion will focus on private property in the sense given by the general notion, but we shall also explicitly consider the consequences that Locke's theory has for the legitimate specification of determinate rights in property. Since we shall refer to individual specific rights by name, there should be no difficulty in identifying which sense is in question on a given occasion.

The Context of Locke's Argument

Throughout our discussion of the interpretation of Locke's argument, we shall be making frequent use of evidence from beyond the text of the *Two Treatises*. The controversiality of this practice will vary, in large measure, according to the provenance of the evidence in question. Where material is adduced from other Locke texts, little controversy is likely to be aroused in principle. Few would dispute, for example, that the argument of a text may be illuminated by the (dis)continuities exhibited when it is read in the context of related antecedent or subsequent discussions by the author, or that the authority of a distinction to elucidate the structure of a text from which it is strictly absent is enhanced if it can be established that the author has articulated the same distinction on another occasion. This is not to suggest, of course, that considerations of this kind will always advance our understanding of a text, but only to recall that they do belong to conventional interpretative practice.

Reference to the broader intellectual context in which a text was written is also a fairly conventional means of facilitating its interpretation. That is, it is largely accepted that the contemporary debates to which the argument of a text contributes, as well as the intellectual tradition(s) within which or in opposition to which its author works, are relevant to our understanding of the argument. To this extent, our appeals in interpreting Locke to features of the seventeenth-century natural law tradition or to the character of the challenge posed by Filmer are unlikely to be overly controversial either.

Considerably greater controversy, however, is engendered by the contention that the interpretation of a text—or, at least, that of a text such as the *Two Treatises*—must (in part) depend on an understanding of the *practical*, that is, social and political, context in which it was written. While this is not a claim we shall advance, it is one that has been made and impressively illustrated by Richard Ashcraft's monumental *Revolutionary Politics and Locke's Two Treatises of Government*.[19] Ashcraft argues that

---

19. Ashcraft's book will hereinafter be abbreviated *RP*. All subsequent internal page cites in this chapter are to *RP*.

> Locke's political theory ... arose within the context of a political movement in which he was a participant, along with thousands of others. The *Two Treatises of Government* was, in effect, the political manifesto of this movement. Much of the meaning of Locke's political theory is thus rooted not only in a particular perception of social reality he shared with others in seventeenth-century England, but it is also tied in rather concrete terms to the specifically political objectives around which large numbers of individuals organised themselves in the 1670s and 1680s under the leadership of the Earl of Shaftesbury. (p. 9)

The interpretation of the *Two Treatises* that Ashcraft offers on the basis of his understanding of this context raises a number of challenging questions. In part, this challenge arises in the domain of interpretative methodology. We shall leave this aspect of Ashcraft's work to one side.[20]

But what is obviously no small part of the challenge is addressed to interpreters of Locke in particular. For those whose interpretation of Locke's theory owes little to a consideration of the practical context in which the *Two Treatises* were written, the nature of this challenge is to relate their interpretation to the one offered by Ashcraft. For those who thereby discover a certain measure of incongruity, there is the further challenge of having to impugn either Ashcraft's understanding of this context or its relevance to the interpretation of Locke's theory. Although Ashcraft's interpretation of Locke is not restricted to the issue of property, a considerable portion of one chapter 'is devoted to an interpretation of the chapter on property in the *Second Treatise*, seen from the vantage point of the kinds of political objectives that guided the Whig political movement in 1680–1681' (p. xiv). The challenge of Ashcraft's work, then, is clearly one of direct concern to us.

I shall maintain that where there are points of significant contact between Ashcraft's account of the practical context in which the *Two Treatises* were written and the interpretation of Locke's theory of property I shall present, Ashcraft's conclusions support my own. As we shall see, there are basically two such points. I shall simply summarise here the elements of Ashcraft's account which are salient in this respect. For the

---

20. For that matter, it should be said that we shall not be taking up any of the methodological questions broached in the previous paragraphs either. The observation that the assumptions underlying our use of certain kinds of evidence in the interpretation of Locke's argument are (relatively) uncontroversial is intended simply to account for this omission and not inadequately to fill it.

most part, this summary will be divided under the headings of the sections in which the corresponding elements of my interpretation are to be presented. The defence of the claim that Ashcraft's conclusions support mine will be taken up in the respective sections themselves.

The general context in which Ashcraft sets the *Two Treatises* is that of the ideological debate that developed during the exclusion crisis of 1679–1681. The focus of this crisis was the question of the succession of the Catholic Duke of York, James, to the English throne. Opposition to James's succession was one of the rallying points of the Whig political movement, to which Locke belonged, as was the advancement of trade and the defence of parliamentary power. The period of the exclusion crisis was also marked by three national elections, and it is in the somewhat narrower context of the Whig electoral campaigns that Ashcraft situates his discussion of Locke's theory of property.

In particular, what Ashcraft wants to show is the appeal as election propaganda that the various arguments advanced by the Whigs in the exclusion debate had in relation to specific socioeconomic groups. The heart of the Whig political movement was drawn from 'the trading part of the nation' (p. 231), but their election strategy sought 'to forge an alliance between merchants, tradesmen, artisans, shopkeepers, *and* yeoman farmers and the gentry' (p. 228). This last group assumed a special importance because 'the practical success of the Whig political movement—certainly as far as the electoral process was concerned—depended upon their winning a significant part of the gentry over to their side' (p. 243). Winning the support of the gentry, Ashcraft maintains, turned on the Whigs' ability to alienate the gentry from three segments of society: from the Crown, from the influence of the Anglican clergy, and from the landowning aristocracy. It is only the third of these objectives that will be of interest to us here.

The Consent Problem

On Ashcraft's analysis, property was 'next to the attack upon the clergy through a critique of Filmer... the most important and troublesome issue for the Whigs in their effort to gain the support of the gentry' (p. 246). The difficulty of this issue stemmed from the concern that members of the gentry had for the security of their property rights: if the security of these property rights were perceived to be jeopardised by a Whig victory, the Whigs would stand little chance of gaining the support of the gentry. Ashcraft emphasises two factors which contributed to this perception. First, there were the claims of the Whigs' political opponents, the Tories, for whom the point was something of a propaganda boon. The Tories

> argued that the ten thousand manors of the gentry depended upon the maintenance of the King's (Charles II's) authority, and they threatened the gentry with the loss of their property if the Whigs were successful in weakening that authority, and perhaps, in establishing a republic. The result would be a 'levelling' of men's estates. (p. 246)

Second, the Whigs' 'increasing reliance upon the language of natural rights and the state of nature seemed to push [them] toward the assertion that property had originally been held in common' (p. 255). Notwithstanding the traditional character of this assertion, its contemporary connotations were such as to raise doubts about the security of existing property relations in Whig hands. 'Whatever we may think, for Englishmen in the 1680's, the authority of Grotius or the early Christian fathers did not simply set aside the tarnishment this proposition had received from having been incorporated into a number of Leveller and Digger tracts in the 1640's' (p. 255n).

Thus, given the prominent role accorded to the gentry in the Whig election strategy, it evidently behoved the Whigs to dispel the perception that their principles were inhospitable to the security of property. In order to do this, they 'needed some means of reconciling the language of equality, natural rights, and the view that all property was originally given to mankind "in common" with a justification of individual property rights' (p. 251). Moreover, this reconciliation had to be a genuine one, since the language of natural rights could only be abandoned 'at the price of alienating the Whig supporters among artisans and tradesmen, for whom such appeals and language found a very sound resonance' (p. 252). Accordingly, Ashcraft concludes, 'if a practical alliance between the country gentry and the urban tradesmen was to be effected, . . . the theoretical problem of property rights had to be confronted and resolved in a manner that would satisfy both groups' (p. 252).

Rights and the Means of Preservation

The practical alliance that the Whigs hoped to create can be understood, in relation to the position of the gentry, as both a positive and a negative construction. As a positive construction, it represents a recognition of the common (commercial) interests shared by the gentry and the more traditional Whig constituency. As a negative construction, it represents the alienation of the gentry from, inter alia, the landowning aristocracy. Ashcraft argues that Locke's theory of property provides a basis for advocating the construction of such an alliance in both positive and negative terms. What is more, this is held to be deliberate. 'The chapter on property in the *Second Treatise* . . . has precisely this intentional objective: to provide a defense of "the industrious" and trading part of the nation—the constituency to whom the Whigs addressed their appeals—against the idle, unproductive, and Court-dominated property owners' (p. 264).[21]

The basis in question is derived from a 'socially rooted conception of labour and property that Locke, at least from the time of his association with the Earl of Shaftesbury, incorporated into his understanding of political society,' a conception that 'supplies a positive endorsement of labouring activity, productivity, and commercial expansion, and a corresponding critique of idleness and waste' (p. 266). In its light, individuals who labour are seen as contributing to the public good and, on Ashcraft's account, this evaluative standard serves to buttress advocacy of the alliance sought by the Whigs.

In positive terms, this standard upholds the activities of the members of that alliance as contributions to the public good, while in negative terms it sets the idle element of the landowning aristocracy apart as failing to make such a contribution.[22] The locus of this buttress in Locke's theory is found, according to Ashcraft, in its identification of *labour* as

---

21. Ashcraft explains that 'by comprehending the labor employed to cultivate and enclose acreage under the general label of "the industrious"' (p. 244), the Whigs were able to deploy this term as a description of their (would-be) alliance.

22. In fact, Ashcraft suggests that 'Locke's chapter on property is one of the most radical critiques of the [useless] landowning aristocracy produced during the last half of the seventeenth century' (p. 273).

the title to property (pp. 257 and 262). Given this identification, he concludes, 'the political message of the chapter was clear enough: Artisans, small gentry, yeoman farmers, tradesmen and merchants were all productive members of society and ought, therefore, to unite in pursuit of their interests against an idle and wasteful landowning aristocracy' (p. 281).

Overview

My discussion is divided into two parts, consisting of two chapters each. Part I concerns the interpretation of Locke's theory of property. In chapter 2, I introduce the consent problem and discuss the operation of the core structure of Locke's theory subsequent to the introduction of money in the state of nature. I criticise various current interpretations of the consequences of land scarcity in this connection and present Locke's solution to the consent problem. In chapter 3, I argue for the interpretation of Locke's labour mixture metaphor in terms of the maker's right doctrine. I complete this part of the discussion with a brief account of the transition to civil society.

Part II addresses the question of the kind of private property right that can actually be established with this argument. In chapter 4, I discuss the kind of property right that follows from the argument as presented in the *Two Treatises*, beginning with Locke's conclusions in this regard and proceeding to my own investigation of this question. In so doing I seek to redress the first respect in which Locke's own theory is an imperfect instance of a Lockean theory of property. In chapter 5, I consider a contemporary version of the Lockean argument which does not incorporate the extraneous elements of the argument in the *Two Treatises*. This allows me not only to redress the second respect in which Locke's theory is imperfectly Lockean, but also to determine the kind of private property right that can still be established on Lockean grounds.

I close my discussion by reviewing the principal conclusions of its respective parts as well as the principal arguments that have been offered in their defence.

I

Property in the *Two Treatises*

2

Property without Consent

John Locke's classic treatment of the question of property is presented in chapter 5 of his *Second Treatise of Government*. For Locke, as for his seventeenth-century contemporaries, *the* question of property is the problem of acquisition. Agreement on this single problem, Richard McKeon has argued, distinguishes the writing of this period from traditional discussions of property—oriented to the twin problems of acquisition and of use, in the case of Plato and Aristotle, and only to the problem of use in the case of medieval thinkers—and constitutes the hallmark of modern theories of property.[1]

Natural Law and Natural Rights

Although the debate about property in which Locke and his contemporaries participated was shaped by a concern we continue to share, the same cannot be said for the idiom in terms of which this debate was conducted. Locke writes in the language of seventeenth-century natural law and natural rights discourse and his theory of property is informed by the intellectual matrix constituted by that tradition.[2]

---

1. R. McKeon, 'The Development of the Concept of Private Property in Political Philosophy: A Study of the Background of the Constitution,' *Ethics* 48 (1937), pp. 343–44.
2. J. Tully, *A Discourse on Property: John Locke and His Adversaries* (Cambridge: Cambridge University Press, 1980), p. ix. Tully's book will hereinafter be abbreviated *DP*.

22   *Property in the* Two Treatises

The starting point for the analysis of property in this natural law tradition is the common right which men have in all things.³ Grotius, Pufendorf, Suárez, John Selden, and Richard Cumberland all proceed from this shared point of reference.⁴ Locke is thus on familiar ground in opening chapter 5 with the declaration that

> [w]hether we consider natural Reason, which tells us, that Men, being once born, have a right to their Preservation, and consequently to Meat and Drink, and such other things, as Nature affords for their Subsistence: or Revelation, which gives us an account of those Grants God made of the World to Adam, and to Noah, and his Sons, 'tis very clear, that God, as King David says, Psal. CXV.xvi. has given the Earth to the Children of Men, given to Mankind in common. (II, 25)

That this is a familiar proposition does not excuse Locke from having to provide an argument for it. Locke's argument begins from the premiss that men are 'all the Workmanship of one Omnipotent, and infinitely wise Maker; All the Servants of one Sovereign Master, sent into the World by his order and about his business' (II, 6). As Peter Laslett observes, 'to John Locke this was a proposition of common sense, the initial proposition of a work which appeals to common sense throughout.'⁵ From the fact that God created man to do his bidding, it must be concluded that God intended for man to be preserved and 'not that so curious and wonderful a piece of Workmanship by its own Negligence or want of Necessaries, should perish again, presently after a few moments continuance' (I, 86). This conclusion is reinforced by rational consideration of the strong desire of self-preservation which God has planted in man as a principle of action: 'Reason, which was the voice of God in him, could not but teach him and assure him, that pursuing that natural Inclination he had to preserve his Being, he followed the Will of his Maker' (I, 86). Whence the fundamental law of nature: the preservation of mankind (II, 6; 135).⁶ On Locke's account,

---

3. McKeon, 'Private Property in Political Philosophy,' pp. 344–45.
4. See Tully, *DP*, pp. 64–94.
5. Laslett, Introduction to *Two Treatises of Government*, p. 49.
6. Compare with the extremely similar structure of Locke's derivation of the second law of nature, the preservation of society, in his journal for 15 July 1678: 'If he find that God has made him and all other men in a state wherein they cannot subsist without so-

the original and foundation of all Law is dependency. A dependent intelligent being is under the power and direction and dominion of him on whom he depends and must be for the ends appointed by that superior being. If man were independent he could have no law but his own will no end but himself.[7]

The formal cause of law, in other words, consists in 'the decree of a superior will.'[8] In particular, then, the law of nature 'can be described as being the decree of the divine will discernible by the light of nature.'[9] The prescriptive authority of natural law, of God's will, obtains because man is God's creation, His workmanship, and so is dependent on Him.

> For, ultimately, all obligation leads back to God, and we are bound to show ourselves obedient to the authority of His will because both our being and our work depend on His will, since we have received these from Him, and so we are bound to observe the limits He prescribes.[10]

Hence, the first law of nature imposes a natural duty on mankind: 'Everyone is bound to preserve himself' and, other things being equal, 'to preserve the rest of Mankind' (II, 6). It follows that men have a natural right to preservation (II, 25) and to preserve themselves (II, 11). These two natural rights may be distinguished by considering the particular duty each right imposes on others when possessed by a rights-bearer. In the former case, others have a duty to refrain from directly endangering the

---

ciety and has given them judgement to discern what is capable of preserving and maintaining that society, can he but conclude that he is obliged, and that God requires him to follow those rules which conduce to the preserving of society.' Quoted in Laslett, Introduction to *Two Treatises of Government*, p. 49.

Locke's derivation of a third law of nature, the assignment and rendering of 'praise, honour, and glory' to God, is equally similar. See J. Locke, *Essays on the Law of Nature*, ed. W. von Leyden (Oxford: Clarendon Press, 1954), fourth essay, ff. 59–61, p. 157. References to this work, hereinafter abbreviated *ELN*, give both the folio pagination of Locke's Latin text and the pagination of von Leyden's English translation.

7. Ethica B MS. Locke, c. 28, f. 141. Quoted in Dunn, *Political Thought of John Locke*, p. 1.

8. Locke, *ELN*, first essay, f. 12, pp. 111–13; cf. fourth essay, f. 52, p. 151; ff. 58–59, pp. 155–57; sixth essay, f. 83, pp. 181–83; f. 84, p. 183; and f. 86, p. 185.

9. Locke, *ELN*, first essay, f. 11, p. 111.

10. Locke, *ELN*, sixth essay, f. 84, p. 183; cf. ff. 88–89, p. 187: 'God has created us out of nothing and, if He pleases, will reduce us again to nothing: we are, therefore, subject to Him in perfect justice and by utmost necessity.' For a fuller analysis, see Tully, *DP*, ch. 2, and von Leyden, Introduction to *ELN*, pp. 43–60.

life of the rights-bearer; in the latter case, others have a duty to refrain from impeding the rights-bearer from actively preserving herself.[11]

These two natural rights constitute the ground of the further natural right to property in common. If a man had a right to his preservation and a right to preserve himself, then he had a right to the means of preservation.[12] 'Every Man had a right to the Creatures, by the same Title Adam had, viz. by the right everyone had to take care of, and provide for their Subsistence: and thus Men had a right in common' (I, 87; cf. I, 86, 97; II, 25, 172). Locke's initial community of property is thus an implication of the natural law framework developed elsewhere in the *Two Treatises*.

The Consent Problem

Almost as common to the traditional natural law analysis of property as the initial assumption of property in common is a notorious difficulty to which that assumption gave rise. Man may be endowed communally, but he must be nourished individually.[13] Yet, in taking any particular item from the common, it would seem that a man violates the rights of the other commoners, to whom, *ex hypothesi*, that particular item also belongs. An original community of property therefore appears to be inconsistent with the formation of individual property rights.[14] Consequently,

---

11. Cf. Tully, *DP*, p. 62. Note that these do not exhaust the rights related to preservation.

12. Just precisely in what this right to the means of preservation consists is of some considerable importance to the interpretation of Locke's theory of property. The traditional assumption that it is a right to consume subsistence quantities of 'meat and drink' is difficult to reconcile with the text.

13. The phrase is borrowed from J. Waldron, 'Locke's Account of Inheritance and Bequest,' *Journal of the History of Philosophy* 19 (1981), p. 42; cf. II, 26.

14. Various natural law writers attempt to resolve this problem in various ways. Grotius, for example, famously posits a worldwide compact, in accordance with which individual property expressly arises through universal consent. Tyrrell, on the other hand, replaces the initial positive community of property (everyone owns everything) with an initial negative community (nobody owns anything) and thus obviates the particular problem set by the traditional starting-point. Filmer ridicules the notion of a worldwide compact, which he sees as the only possible solution, and thereby calls into question the assumption of an original community of property. For an excellent discussion, and references, see Tully, *DP*, pp. 64–98.

'this [community] being supposed, it seems to some a very great difficulty, how any one should ever come to have a Property in any thing' (II, 25).

Locke sets himself the task of resolving this difficulty. To be precise, Locke sets himself a somewhat more ambitious task: he wants to demonstrate not simply that his initial community of property can be reconciled with the emergence of individual property rights,[15] but that this can be done without recourse to the mediation of consent. 'But I shall endeavour to shew, how Men might come to have a property in several parts of that which God gave to Mankind in common, and that without any express Compact of all the Commoners' (II, 25). Let us call this more ambitious task the *consent problem*.

In proposing to circumvent the necessity of a compact, Locke signals his intention that his theory of property in the state of nature should stand as a direct refutation of Filmer and thus contribute to the larger polemical purpose for which the *Two Treatises* were written.[16] We may observe here that this is the first of the two points on which Ashcraft's account of the practical context of Locke's argument supports our interpretation. On Ashcraft's account,[17] Locke's larger polemical purpose includes addressing the needs of the Whigs' electoral strategy, in particular to reconcile 'the view that all property was originally given to mankind "in common" with a justification of individual property rights' (*RP*, p. 251), and so his theory must be read as being directed to the consent problem.[18]

Not only does Locke explicitly introduce his theory of property as being directed to this end, but he also concludes what has been called 'part A,

---

15. Grotius' postulate of a worldwide compact would suffice to demonstrate this. This postulate had, however, been thoroughly discredited by Filmer. For an interesting critical discussion of Filmer's argument, see S. Buckle, *Natural Law and the Theory of Property* (Oxford: Clarendon Press, 1991), pp. 162–68.
16. Laslett, ed. note to II, 25, *Two Treatises of Government*, pp. 327–28.
17. See chapter 1, pp. 15–16, of this book.
18. Although Ashcraft does not specifically attribute to the Whigs the need for the more ambitious reconciliation demanded by the consent problem, they obviously did require it. A reconciliation mediated by the assumption of universal consent would have been especially ill-suited to the Whigs' purposes given that it was *Filmer*, the Tory champion, who had so discredited it. On Filmer's status in the political debate of the exclusion crisis, see Ashcraft, *RP*, pp. 186–90.

the theory of appropriation,'[19] of chapter 5 with the implicit claim that he has successfully discharged that task: '[S]upposing the World given as it was to the Children of Men in common, we see how labour could make Men distinct titles to several parts of it, for their private uses' (II, 39).

It is therefore somewhat surprising that the consent problem has received such inadequate attention from Locke's commentators. In many cases, the attention given is completely inadequate: the issue is ignored altogether[20] or, more commonly, it is mentioned summarily and the tacit assumption is made that Locke solves the problem somehow, but it is not explained how.[21] In other cases, the consent problem comes in for more explicit attention, but the attention nevertheless proves inadequate because the solutions attributed to Locke simply, sometimes obviously, will not do. Four putative solutions can be made out from the literature.

The first of these imputes to Locke, against the text, an initial negative community of property.[22] As we have noted, this was the strategy employed by Tyrrell in order to remove the presumption that taking something from the common violated the rights of the other commoners (and hence required their consent). If no one has any rights in the common, then plainly violations of these rights are no longer possible. But for this very reason we may not attribute this solution to Locke, who only raises the consent problem *after* having introduced his initial community of property. His aspiration to circumvent the requirement of consent would make no sense if we read him as having just removed the traditional basis of that requirement.

---

19. K. Olivecrona, 'Locke's Theory of Appropriation,' *Philosophical Quarterly* 24 (96) (1974), p. 220.

20. See A. Ryan, 'Locke and the Dictatorship of the Bourgeoisie,' *Political Studies* 13 (2) (1965), pp. 219-30; G. A. Cohen, *Marx and Locke on Land and Labour* (London: British Academy, 1985); D. Miller, 'Justice and Property,' *Ratio* 22 (1) (1980), pp. 1–14.

21. See Laslett, Introduction to *Two Treatises of Government*, pp. 114–15; E. J. Hundert, 'Market Society and Meaning in Locke's Political Philosophy,' *Journal of the History of Philosophy* 15 (1) (1977), p. 35. Waldron, rather curiously, discusses the issue at some length in *RPP*, pp. 148–57, but then neglects to explain what Locke's solution actually is. He does recognise, however, that it is neither Grotius' solution nor Tyrrell's.

22. See Dunn, *Political Thought of John Locke*, p. 67; A. Ryan, *Property and Political Theory* (Oxford: Basil Blackwell, 1984), p. 30; Buckle, *Natural Law*, pp. 152n, 165, 175, 183–87.

Despite the text, some commentators persist in glossing Locke's initial community as a negative community because of the very broad sense in which they understand *negative community*. Stephen Buckle, for instance, seems to mean by it any community of property in which universal consent is not a necessary condition of removing things from the common.[23] He thus contrasts it with *positive community*, which he understands very narrowly: 'In positive community, all men are joint owners, and so their explicit consent is needed before any part can be removed from the common.'[24] Let us separate the important point here from the purely verbal question. Obviously positive community can be defined so as to preclude a solution to the consent problem,[25] and equally obviously Locke did not assert it in this sense. But knowing this still leaves us without an account of why it is that Locke's commoners are permitted to dispense with the requirement of consent, and that is what was needed. Calling Locke's initial community 'negative' does not alter this fact, unless it misleads us into the false belief that Locke upheld a negative community in the narrow sense that we have associated with Tyrrell.

Conveniently, the next two putative solutions to be examined can both be found in the following discussion of Waldron's.

> It is unnecessary to restate in any detail Locke's argument for the possibility of unilateral acquisition of property entitlements in the state of nature. By 'mixing his labour' with natural resources or pieces of land, a man can acquire such a property in them as to exclude the common right of other men (II, 27 and 32–3). Locke hints at a number of arguments for this position. One of the most important is based on a principle of need: if universal consent were required to legitimate appropriation, then individuals would not be able to take from nature the resources necessary for their survival (I, 86; II, 28).[26]

---

23. 'Those passages [in which he rejects the necessity of consent] *therefore* amount to Locke asserting that the original community must have been negative.' Buckle, *Natural Law*, p. 165; emphasis added.

24. Buckle, *Natural Law*, p. 164.

25. Any definition on which universal consent *is* a necessary condition of removing things from the common will do the trick; cf. Waldron, *RPP*, p. 149.

26. J. Waldron, 'Locke, Tully, and the Regulation of Property,' *Political Studies* 32 (1984), p. 100.

One suggestion that can be discerned here is that appropriation from the common can legitimately proceed without anyone's consent because the annexing of a private right in X to a common right in X excludes or dissolves the common right.[27] Section II, 27, lines 10–13 and II, 32, lines 7–12 do provide prima facie support for this view. But the matter cannot be so simple as all that. On this suggestion, the private right can ride roughshod over the common right. Not only is that not very convincing, but if the mere conjunction with a private right *were* a sufficient solution, it would be difficult to see why the consent problem was so intractable for natural law theorists. In point of fact, Locke adds something vital to this mere conjunction and thereby effects the solution. As we shall see later, it is clear from the continuation of both texts that it is the special context in which this conjunction occurs, rather than the conjunction itself, which circumvents the requirement of consent.

The other suggestion found in this discussion takes Locke's solution of the consent problem to consist in the bare conclusion that universal consent is not a necessary condition of legitimate appropriation.[28] 'If such a consent as that was necessary, Man had starved, notwithstanding the Plenty God had given him' (II, 28). Since consent is not necessary—so the suggestion must go—it may therefore be legitimately forgone.

In fairness to Waldron himself, there is some reason to think that he does not intend this to be construed as an argument for appropriation in the specific context of an initial positive community of property (and so not as a solution to the consent problem).[29] It is nevertheless important, however, to see that Locke's argument here does not solve the consent problem, nor could it have been intended to do so.

Let us begin with the last point. Locke's argument (II, 26, 28) takes the form of a reductio. We shall call it the *paradox of plenty* because the absurdity in which this argument issues is the conclusion that mankind

---

27. Cf. Waldron, *RPP*, p. 155.
28. Buckle's discussion might also be read as involving this suggestion, although he is not very clear about this.
29. In *RPP*, for example, the same argument is reproduced in a section entitled 'Private Property as the Satisfaction of Need.' There (on pp. 168–71), in a context apparently disconnected from his earlier discussion of what we have called the consent problem, this argument is presented and criticised as an argument for private property.

would perish in the midst of the plenty that God had provided for its preservation. The paradox of plenty could serve as a solution to the consent problem only if the initial premiss of the argument were some description of that problem itself, for only then would it be the consent problem from which the absurdity is drawn. But there is no description of the consent problem that is not also a description of the original community of property and that thus does not also equally involve *it* in any alleged absurdity. This was precisely Filmer's point. Since Locke accepts an initial community of property, we cannot suppose that he intends the paradox of plenty as a solution to the consent problem.

It may be easier to see what this argument does not prove if we first establish what it does prove. The paradox of plenty proves that the consent problem can be solved, but it does not itself solve the problem. The initial premiss of the paradox is the assumption that universal consent is the unique sufficient condition of legitimate appropriation from the common. This is the assumption that Locke reduces to absurdity. Reason tells us that the world has been given to man for his use; therefore there must be *some* way to individuate the common.[30] If universal consent is the only way to do so, then it is a necessary condition of individuating the common. But, 'if such a consent as that was necessary, Man had starved, notwithstanding the Plenty God had given him' (II, 28). Hence, consent is not necessary. Hence, there *must* be at least one other (legitimate) individuating procedure. This proves that the consent problem can be solved.

Notice that it does not follow that *any* other individuating procedure would be legitimate. The commoners still have rights which are not dissolved by the existence of nonconsensual individuation. Nothing in the argument sanctions the violation of common rights. Notice too that the argument does not specify what this other procedure is. It only says that at least one such procedure exists. Thus, the paradox of plenty manifestly is not a solution to the consent problem: a solution would both specify the nonconsensual procedure and explain why it is legitimate.

---

30. 'Yet being given for the use of Men, there must of necessity be a means to appropriate them some way or other before they can be of any use, or at all beneficial to any particular Man' (II, 26).

The fourth and last putative solution of the consent problem that we shall examine is offered by James Tully—one of the few commentators who does take the consent problem seriously[31]—in his *A Discourse on Property: John Locke and His Adversaries*. Central to Tully's interpretation of Locke's solution is a distinction drawn by C. B. Macpherson between an exclusive and an inclusive right. An exclusive right confers the right to exclude others from that to which the right refers; an inclusive right confers the right to be included in, that is, not to be excluded from, that to which the right refers. What Locke's commoners possess, Tully holds, is an inclusive natural right: a right not to be excluded from the use of the common—the earth, the inferior creatures, and so on.

The common belongs to everyone to use to acquire the means necessary for comfort and support. But heed must be paid to the referent of this inclusive natural right. 'Locke's property is . . . a right to one's *due* rather than to one's *own*' (p. 61).[32] That is, the right refers to one's *share* of the means necessary for comfort and support. 'Thus, each right does not refer to every item on the common. Indeed, it does not refer to any item on the common but, rather, to items made from the common. . . . Since each man has a right to his due share and no more, acquisition of it cannot be robbery'(p. 127). On this interpretation, then, 'Locke's solution, like Cumberland's, is to redefine positive community' (p. 127).

In fact, Tully presses his claim further and suggests that 'Locke effects an important conceptual clarification in his analysis of natural property and belonging to everyone in common' (p. 128). Traditionally, both a right and its referent were called property. Applied to a common right, this practice carries the implication that the whole common is property. It is to avoid this implication, according to Tully, that Locke 'moves to a more careful analysis of the object of a common right' (p. 128). Accordingly, the referent of Locke's inclusive common right is a share of the

---

31. It would be remiss not to acknowledge at least that, in his recent book, John Simmons also takes the consent problem seriously, especially since one of the solutions he affirms is similar to the one we shall defend. He also appears to affirm as solutions the argument we have called the paradox of plenty and a variant of the redefinition of positive community proposed by Tully. See J. Simmons, *The Lockean Theory of Rights* (Princeton: Princeton University Press, 1992), pp. 236–41.

32. This and subsequent internal page cites in this chapter to Tully are to *DP*.

common and not the common itself. This represents a conceptual clarification: 'To refrain from predicating "property" of that which belongs to everyone in common saves this important concept from reduction to property in several' (p. 128).

One consequence of this redefinition and clarification is that robbery can no longer be defined as taking what belongs to another, but must now be understood as taking more than one's share. Here Tully adduces statements from Locke such as 'else he took more than his share, and robb'd others' (II, 46).

But, while it has certain merits, this interpretation must ultimately be judged unsuccessful, at least as an interpretation of Locke. It is true that the proposed solution does resolve the consent problem nicely (perhaps even more nicely than Locke's own solution) and also allows for greater conceptual precision. The difficulty is that there is no good reason for reading it in the text and at least two good reasons for not doing so.

Understanding the referent of the common right to be a share, as opposed to any or every item on the common, is the crux of the proposed solution. Yet not a single reference is supplied to indicate where in the text Locke makes this crucial move. The only direct textual references given at all have to do with the redefinition of robbery and the exceeding of one's share. On examination, none of these three passages (II, 31, 37, 46) will bear Tully's interpretation. In each of the three passages, the share in question is defined or bounded by the limits of what a man can *use*, commonly known as the spoilage limitation. This contrasts sharply with the requirements of Tully's account: '"Things necessary for comfort and support" is a natural definition of the share which ought to belong to each' (p. 127). Just how sharply is manifested subsequent to the introduction of money, when the shares defined by these two criteria diverge rapidly.

So the first good reason for not reading Locke in this way is that if Locke had been attempting to achieve his main aim through a redefinition of positive community, he surely would have signalled somehow that that was what he was doing. Subtlety in argumentation is a virtue, but there are limits.

The second good reason is that not only is there an absence of any positive, direct support for this interpretation in the text, but the text actually contradicts Tully's reading at a number of points. Recall that the conceptual clarification brought on by the redefinition was the distinction between the referent of a common right (a share) and the common itself. It was only in the former that a commoner had a right and thus only the former was 'property.' This clarification was effected because Locke 'moved to a more careful analysis' and 'refrained from predicating "property"' of the common itself. However, at II, 29 Locke writes, for example, 'Though *the Water* running in the Fountain *be every ones*,' and at II, 30, 'Thus this Law of reason makes *the Deer*, that Indian's who hath killed it; . . . though before, it was the *common right of every one*' (emphases added). 'One's own' and 'right' are both locutions equivalent to 'property,' as Tully himself recognises elsewhere (pp. 113–15). Locke simply cannot be taken to have resolved a traditional problem through a careful redefinition whose strictures he did not himself observe.

In sum, then, we still lack an adequate account of Locke's solution of the consent problem. To explain how Locke solves this problem, however, we shall need to develop some understanding of the core structure of his theory of property. More specifically, we can put ourselves in a better position to appreciate Locke's solution by coming to understand how that structure operates in a context of land scarcity.

The Bare Structure

At the heart of Locke's foundation of property is the famous metaphor of labour mixture, which is set down in the following well-known passage:

> Though the Earth, and all inferior Creatures be common to all Men, yet every Man has a Property in his own Person. This no Body has any Right to but himself. The Labour of his Body and the Work of his Hands, we may say, are properly his. Whatsoever then he removes out of the State that Nature hath provided, and left it in, he hath mixed his Labour with, and joyned to it something that is his own, and thereby makes it his Property. (II, 27)

Labour, according to Locke, gives title to property (II, 45; 34) and thus his theory is known as a labour theory of property. Formally, a *property* in Locke is anything which cannot be taken from a man without his consent (II, 193 and 138; cf. II, 139, 140, 142, 192, 194). Now it is a matter of some controversy just why it is, on Locke's view, that labour confers property. It is controversial, that is, what explanation Locke offers of labour's power to legitimate appropriation. I shall discuss this question at length in chapter 3. For the moment, I shall simply present the traditional interpretation of Locke's explanation of this point and then proceed to the other core elements of Locke's theory.

On the traditional interpretation, the property a man is said to have in his person and in his labour enter Locke's argument as premises, in the sense that these properties are taken to be unargued. Together they are sometimes gathered under the rubric of the 'thesis of self-ownership.'[33] By then mixing this thing that he owns (labour) with an object lying in common, a man comes thereby to have a property in that object.[34] His new property obtains in virtue of the fact that something he already owns is irretrievably mixed with the object in question. Since a ploughed field, say, cannot be taken from a man without also taking from him the labour he expended in ploughing it, the field cannot be taken from him without his consent, any more than that labour could be. But this is just to say that he also has a property in the ploughed field.

Since man has within him the foundation of property (II, 44), it might be feared that he is therefore at liberty to appropriate without limit. 'To which I Answer, Not so. The same Law of Nature, that does by this means give us Property, does also bound that Property too' (II, 31). Locke thus reiterates the principle that liberty is not licence (II, 6). Property exists within and so is bound by a prior framework of natural laws and natural rights. Man's property rights derive from his right to use the common

---

33. See, e.g., Cohen, *Marx and Locke*, pp. 357–59. Sometimes, the property a man has in his labour is said to follow from the property he has in his person. Olivecrona defines property in such a way as to make ownership of one's person an analytic feature of property. 'Locke's Theory of Appropriation,' pp. 221–25.

34. Olivecrona, 'Locke's Theory of Appropriation,' pp. 224–27, advances a variant of the traditional interpretation in which property obtains in virtue of 'an infusion of one's personality.' Notice that the logic of the argument is such that almost anything (personality, magic dust, etc.) can be substituted for labour as long as it is the agent's property. This serves to highlight the non-privileged position of the specific nature of labour in this view.

for the comfort and support of his being (I, 86, 92), from which it follows that his appropriation is limited to what he can use.[35]

> As much as any one can make use of to any advantage of life before it spoils; so much he may by his labour fix a Property in. Whatever is beyond this, is more than his share, and belongs to others. Nothing was made by God for Man to spoil or destroy. (II, 31)

This proviso is traditionally known as the *spoilage limitation*. Spoilage concerns animals and the spontaneous products of nature directly (II, 37), and concerns land indirectly, through the spoilage of the products of the improved land (II, 38).

Locke is also traditionally read as imposing a second proviso on appropriation, known as the *sufficiency limitation*. This reading is principally motivated by the conclusion of II, 27: 'For this labour being the unquestionable Property of the Labourer, no Man but he can have a right to what that is once joyned to, at least where there is enough, and as good left in common for others.' That a man leave enough and as good as that on which he laboured for the use of others is thus a condition of labouring's giving rise to a property in the product.

The bare structure of Locke's theory can accordingly be represented by the following claim: in the state of nature, men can—subject to two provisos—legitimately acquire individual property rights in things by labouring on the common. These provisos are, first, that a man appropriate only as much as he can use before it spoils and, second, that he leave enough and as good for others. This constitutes only the bare structure of the theory because it omits any explanation of either the legitimating power of labour or the operation of the two provisos.

The operation of the provisos stands in need of explanation because it is not clear, for example, whether what the second proviso requires appropriators to leave behind for others is enough and as good as the others had before or merely as what they take themselves. Nor is it clear whether what has to be left behind for others has to be left *in kind*, that is, whether one has to leave enough and as good *land* behind if one is labouring on land. Indeed, it has even been doubted that Locke does

---

35. Nozick, *ASU*, pp. 175–76, cannot see the point of this proviso because he abstracts from the natural law framework which is the context of Locke's discussion.

impose two provisos on appropriation, rather than one.[36] We can turn to these matters straightaway, since I have deferred discussion of the other part of the bare structure until the next chapter. We begin with the spoilage limitation.

Money and Scarcity

Locke's state of nature is periodic rather than static. To be precise, it is marked by two periods, which Karl Olivecrona has called the age of abundance and the age of scarcity.[37] The historical catalyst that effects the transition from abundance to scarcity is the introduction of money.

In the age of abundance, the spoilage limitation and the finitude of labour effectively guarantee that more than enough land will be available for all, the appropriation of some notwithstanding.

> The Measure of Property, Nature has well set, by the Extent of Mens Labour, and the Conveniency of Life. No Mans Labour could subdue, or appropriate all: nor could his Enjoyment consume more than a small part. ... This measure did confine every Man's Possession, to a very moderate Proportion. (II, 36)

Men, Locke suggests, were 'more in danger to be lost' than to be 'straitned for want of room to plant in' (II, 36).

This situation changes with the advent of money because money is imperishable and thus unaffected by the spoilage limitation. Expanding one's property in land is thus made consistent with that limitation by the possibility of exchanging surplus produce, which would otherwise spoil, for money, which will not (II, 46–8, 50). As money may be accumulated indefinitely without violating the spoilage limitation, so too now may land; 'the exceeding of the bounds of his just Property not lying in the largeness of his Possessions, but the perishing of anything uselessly in it' (II, 46). Hence, inexorably, the use of money leads to a scarcity of land (II, 36, 45, 48).

---

36. See J. Waldron, 'Enough and as Good Left for Others,' *Philosophical Quarterly* 29 (1979), pp. 319–28.
37. Olivecrona, 'Locke's Theory of Appropriation,' p. 220. The labels refer to the general availability of land.

In addition to scarcity of land, the use of money also makes possible the 'disproportionate and unequal Possession of the Earth' (II, 50).[38] More accurately, it makes possible *exaggerated* inequality. Previously, disparities were attenuated by the fact that the absolute size of any and all holdings was necessarily 'a very moderate Proportion.' But now, 'as different degrees of Industry were apt to give Men Possession in different Proportions, . . . this Invention of Money gave them the opportunity to continue to enlarge them' (II, 48).

Clearly, Locke sees the adoption of money as a consensual practice, either explicitly—'Men had agreed, that a little piece of yellow Metal, which would keep without wasting or decay, should be worth a great piece of Flesh, or a whole heap of corn' (II, 37; cf. II, 45–7)—or implicitly— 'by putting a value on gold and silver and tacitly agreeing in the use of Money' (II, 50; cf. II, 36). Hence, there is no question but that both scarcity and inequality were *achieved* legitimately, that is, were brought about by fair means. In money, mankind had 'by a tacit and voluntary consent found out a way, how a man may fairly possess more land than he himself can use the product of' (II, 50).

But the controversial question is whether the scarcity occasioned by this legitimate process is itself legitimate.[39] On the face of it, scarcity of land blatantly offends against the sufficiency limitation—where some have no land, it is clear that 'enough and as good' has not been left for others. One is therefore inclined to suppose that such scarcity undermines the legitimacy of the natural property regime because the rights acquired in land were held on the condition that enough and as good is left for others.

Evidently, then, the question of the implication of land scarcity—a question of fundamental importance for Locke's theory—turns on one's understanding of the sufficiency limitation. The traditional view, as we

---

38. These two consequences of the introduction of money are distinct and independent.

39. Inequality per se is perfectly legitimate on any reading of Locke (II, 46, 48). Where its legitimacy is in question, the reasoning is dependent on that of the case of scarcity. The issue at hand has no direct bearing on a similar well-known claim made by Nozick, *ASU*, pp. 151 ff., because, inter alia, the original just distribution here is only conditionally, rather than unconditionally, just.

have said, is that Locke imposes the sufficiency limitation as a necessary condition on appropriation. But it also holds that Locke takes the legitimacy of the system of natural property rights in land to be compatible with scarcity of land. These positions are mediated by the traditional contention that, according to Locke, it is also possible for the sufficiency (and not just the spoilage) limitation to be superseded, although the manner in which this is said to occur is subject to debate.[40]

Tully also holds to the sufficiency limitation as set out above, yet—notoriously—he argues that the structure of Locke's argument 'necessarily invalidates all exclusive rights once the proviso is no longer met' (p. 165). Waldron, on the other hand, accepts the legitimacy of the natural property regime under conditions of scarcity. Instead, he rejects the sufficiency limitation. In his article 'Enough and as Good Left for Others,' he maintains 'that the traditional interpretation is strained and artificial, that Locke did *not* intend the clause to be taken as a restriction or a necessary condition on appropriation'(p. 320).[41]

In short, the issue of the legitimacy of Locke's natural property regime in the age of scarcity may be resolved into three subissues. First, does Locke impose a sufficiency limitation on natural appropriation? Second, if so, is it compatible with scarcity of land? Finally, if so, how?

Since Waldron's critique addresses the point which is logically most prior, it is with his argument that I begin.

Waldron's Critique

Waldron's article presents a powerful challenge to the received reading of Locke. On his interpretation, the 'enough and as good' clause does not restrict appropriation in the least and as such poses no difficulties of legitimacy for the advent of scarcity. Rather, that there *is* enough and as good left in common for others is merely '*a fact about* appropriation in the early ages of man' (p. 322).

---

40. See, e.g., T. Baldwin, 'Tully, Locke, and Land,' *The Locke Newsletter* 13 (1982), pp. 27–29.
41. Subsequent internal page cites in this chapter to Waldron are to 'Enough and as Good.'

In support of this radical claim, Waldron marshalls four arguments. These are, respectively, that Locke does not introduce the clause in the manner of a restriction; that the clause is naturally read as a sufficient rather than as a necessary condition; that Locke does not mention it among the restrictions superseded by the introduction of money; and that reading it as a restriction leads to an absurdity.

We shall argue that the first argument fails to secure the required conclusion; that the second argument is in part correct and tells against the standard understanding of the clause (as does the first, to some extent); that the third argument is correct, but beside the point; and that the fourth argument adduces irrelevant considerations and thus fails.

Waldron bases his first argument on a comparison with Locke's introduction of the spoilage limitation. He argues that it is clear from the use of the language of restraint—'Law of Nature . . . does also bound that Property'—that II, 31 introduces a restriction on appropriation and that this contrasts with II, 27. Moreover, it is suggested that 'Locke writes here as though the spoilage proviso was the *only* restriction on appropriation' (p. 320) and that this is difficult to reconcile with the hypothesis that, four sections earlier, another restriction had been introduced. This is all the more so because Waldron finds in Locke a 'usual practice in the *Second Treatise* of introducing sets of restrictions and conditions in a clearly enumerated order' (p. 321).

However, only by presupposing that the language of II, 27 is not restrictive can a meaningful contrast in this respect be sustained.[42] So this cannot be an independent argument. What does require explanation is Locke's seeming to ignore a restriction he is supposed to have introduced only four sections earlier. Waldron's own supplementary point regarding sets of restrictions provides the key. Locke enumerates restrictions in sets when they are of a piece, that is, all of the same order. For example, the restrictions on the legislature that Waldron mentions all issue from the same source, namely, the 'trust that is put in them by the Society, and the Law of God and Nature' (II, 142).

---

42. Waldron surely cannot intend the absence of a specific word such as 'restrict' or 'limit' in II, 27 to be significant.

The spoilage limitation issues directly from the law of nature. As we have seen, a right of use is the only kind of property which can arise in the particular natural law framework from which Locke begins. Thus, we might say that the spoilage limitation is an absolute limitation. It cannot be overridden, not even by consent: 'Nothing was made by God for Man to spoil or destroy' (II, 31).

Locke's failure to mention the sufficiency limitation in the same breath means little more than that it is not an absolute limitation. After all, it is not as if Locke simply ignores the consideration of sufficiency after introducing it in II, 27. He reiterates the point frequently enough in 'Part A' of chapter 5 to establish that it plays some role—just what remains to be seen—in his argument (II, 33–7). In fact, this sufficiency consideration is present even in II, 31, the section on which Waldron bases his objection ('And thus considering the Plenty of natural Provisions'). Waldron obscures this fact by his selective quotation of the passage.

It follows, then, that it is wrong to treat the sufficiency and spoilage limitations as though they are on the same footing, as many traditional accounts are wont to do. But it certainly does not follow that the 'enough and as good' clause is not restrictive. This much should be obvious anyhow from the fact that consent may dissolve the sufficiency but not the spoilage limitation.

Waldron's second argument focuses on the 'rather ambiguous logical connective' *at least where*, which introduces Locke's phrase 'at least where there is enough, and as good left in common for others' (II, 27). He contends that the natural reading of this connective is as introducing a sufficient rather than a necessary condition. Thus, properly read, the phrase holds that labour certainly gives rise to a property where enough and as good is left in common for others, and perhaps even where it is not (p. 321). To some extent, this suggestion is compelling.

Notice, however, that Waldron tacitly assumes here that what is left in common is left *in kind*. So, for the central case of land, Waldron's suggestion is that a property in land relevantly obtains certainly where enough and as good *land* is left in common, and perhaps even where there is not enough and as good *land* left in common. Read thus, Waldron's point is well taken and, again, tells against the standard reading.

But it falls well short of establishing that Locke is not here restricting appropriation in any way. What would be required for that much stronger conclusion is a supplementary clause in the expansion, namely, 'and perhaps *even where no thing* enough and as good is left in common for others.' There is nothing in Waldron's argument that warrants this extreme licence. Just because appropriation may be legitimate in cases where enough and as good *land* is not left in common does not mean that there are therefore *no* restrictions of sufficiency on appropriation.

We shall ignore the third argument for the moment, although elements of it will enter the discussion later. The reason for this is that its conclusion—that Locke does not number the sufficiency limitation among the restrictions circumvented by the introduction of money—only bears on the issue at hand on the unwarranted (or at least yet to be decided) assumption that all original restrictions are in fact circumvented by the introduction of money.

The fourth argument is that if the sufficiency limitation were a necessary condition on appropriation, then in a counterfactual situation of original scarcity instead of plenty everyone would starve, in contravention of natural law—an evident absurdity. What is omitted here is the recognition that Locke's natural law framework is derived in a context of plenty, which enters substantially into that derivation (cf. I, 86 and II, 28). Waldron's counterfactual can have no purchase with natural law so derived. In spite of this, moreover, the argument is open to the now familiar objection that 'absolute restriction' and 'absence of restriction' do not exhaust the relevant possibilities.

Waldron is therefore correct to say that the enough and as good clause, unlike the spoilage proviso, is not a natural law limitation imposing an absolute restriction on appropriation.[43] It is a mistake, though, to suppose on this basis that Locke does not impose a sufficiency limitation of any kind on natural appropriation. The strongest and most satisfactory way to make good on this claim is to provide a coherent and convincing account of the limitation actually imposed by the enough and as good clause.

---

43. Even subsequent to the introduction of money, the spoilage limitation formally imposes an absolute restriction on appropriation, though its practical effect may be negligible.

Rights and the Means of Preservation

Locke's account of property begins from the natural right man has to property in common. This right, which is derived from the natural right a man has to his preservation and to preserve himself, is the same as the right to the means of preservation.[44] The property rights men subsequently acquire through labour all flow from this right to the means of preservation.[45] Thus, property in labour's product may be seen as the actualisation of a prior right to the means of preservation. The content of this right is therefore of considerable importance.

Now, on any interpretation, the right to the means of preservation must ultimately issue in a right to *consume* subsistence quantities of meat, drink, and whatnot; otherwise, it could not serve to bring about the preservation of mankind. The traditional account, however, fixes on an absolutely literal reading of a passage in II, 25 in order to conclude that the right to the means of preservation is *itself*, immediately, just this consumption right: 'Men, being once born, have a right to their Preservation, and consequently to Meat and Drink, and such other things as nature affords for their Subsistence.' According to this interpretation, there are three distinct ways in which one's right to the means of preservation can be exercised—through labour, charity, or inheritance.[46] Use of the traditional reading is most evident in discussions of Locke's treatment of charity.

The implication of the traditional discussion of charity in Locke is that need as such is sufficient to actualise this consumption right; that anyone who, through poverty or misfortune, possesses no meat, drink, or

---

44. 'God, I say, having made Man and the World thus, spoke to him, (that is) directed him by his Senses and Reason . . . to the use of those things, which were serviceable for his Subsistence, and given him as means of his Preservation' (I, 86; cf. I, 87, 97; II, 25, 172).

45. 'Property, whose Original is from the Right a Man has to use any of the Inferior Creatures, for the Subsistence and Comfort of his Life' (I, 92; cf. I, 86).

46. Tully, *DP*, p. 131.

whatnot has a *right* to be provided with subsistence quantities of the same.[47] Thus, Waldron holds that, on Locke's theory, special rights of property 'are themselves constrained by a deeper and, in the last resort, more powerful *general* right which each man has to the material necessaries for his survival. This forms the basis of what one might refer to as entitlements of charity in Locke's system' (*RPP*, p. 39). Similarly, Tully finds in Locke 'a prior inclusive claim right to provisions, though not to raw materials, necessary for subsistence' (p. 123).

Taken to its logical conclusion, the traditional interpretation suggests that one's right to consume subsistence quantities of meat and drink is strictly independent of one's labouring. This is, in fact, exactly the position advocated by Ashcraft in his *Locke's Two Treatises of Government*: 'Therefore, not only is it true that we are each responsible for securing the right of everyone to subsistence, but it is also true that this rights claim is *not* tied to the labour of the individual or framed in terms of it.'[48] As the basis of this inference, Ashcraft adduces the following passage from Locke's proposal for reforming the poor law: 'Everyone must have meat, drink, clothing, and firing. So much goes out of the stock of the kingdom, whether they work or no.'[49]

We shall argue that the traditional interpretation of the right to the means of preservation—and so, a fortiori, Ashcraft's position—should be set aside in favour of another interpretation. Before we do so, however, it will be convenient first to dispose of the one, specious piece of evidence that Ashcraft offers for his position. The plausibility of this passage as evidence for that position is entirely due to its being quoted out of context; even then, we may note that no mention is there made of *rights*. But in its context, it is clear that Locke decidedly does not mean that everyone has a right to meat, drink, and whatnot, even if he does not

---

47. Cf. Waldron, 'Locke's Account of Inheritance,' p. 45: 'since, if Locke is right here, extreme want gives rise to a full-blooded property entitlement, it follows that a Lockean government is not only permitted to run some sort of welfare system, financed by taxation, but actually *obliged* to do so. . . .'

48. R. Ashcraft, *Locke's Two Treatises of Government* (London: Allen and Unwin, 1987), p. 127.

49. J. Locke, *A Report to the Board of Trade to the Lords Justices 1697, Respecting Relief and Unemployment of the Poor*, in H. R. Fox Bourne, *The Life of John Locke*, vol. 2 (London: Henry S. King, 1876), p. 382.

work; indeed, his proposed reforms could scarcely have had a more contrary objective.

Locke's brief in making his proposal was 'to consider of some proper methods for setting on work and employing the poor of this kingdom, and making them useful to the public, and thereby easing others of that burden.'[50] His aim in the paragraph whose first two lines are quoted by Ashcraft is to illustrate the fiscal advantages of his proposal (compulsory employment of all those seeking relief 'as far as they are able to work') as compared with then-current practice (on which recipients of relief are 'maintained in idleness'). The passage in question represents an accounting of the common costs of the two schemes, his ('they work') and the then-current one ('or no'); the remainder of the paragraph represents an accounting of the revenues which will accrue on his scheme only.[51] Locke presents the conclusion to be drawn from his illustration in the very next paragraph: 'This, rightly considered, shows us what is the true and proper relief of the poor. It consists in finding work for them, and taking care that they do not live like drones upon the labour of others.' There is no basis in this text for Ashcraft's position.

It is submitted that Locke's right to the means of preservation is itself a right to *produce* subsistence quantities of meat, drink, and whatnot—that is, a right not to be excluded from the use of the common materials which have been plentifully provided by God and from which the direct means of support can be produced. An inclusive right of this sort may be thought of as a right of access: no right-bearer may be denied access to the common materials necessary to produce 'Food and Rayment, etc.': 'So that here was no Priviledge of his Heir above his other Children, which could exclude them from an equal Right to the use of the inferior Crea-

---

50. Quoted passages in this paragraph appear in Locke, *Report to the Board of Trade*, pp. 377, 382–83.

51. The remainder reads as follows: '. . . they work or no. Supposing then there be a hundred thousand poor in England, that live upon the parish, that is, who are maintained by other people's labour (for so is everyone who lives upon alms without working), if care were taken that every one of these, by some labour in the woollen or other manufacture, should earn but a penny per diem (which, one with another, they might well do and more), this would gain to England 130,000 l. per annum, which, in eight years, would make England above a million pounds richer.'

tures, for the comfortable preservation of their Being, which is all the Property Man hath in them' (I, 87).

Since, as Locke argues, production of something from the common materials provided by God entitles one to a property in that thing, and since property in something clearly embraces a right to consume that thing,[52] this production right does also issue in a right to consume subsistence quantities of meat, drink, and whatnot. But the production right is not to be identified with the consumption right. The distinction between this and the traditional interpretation centres on the point that here the issuance of a man's right to the means of preservation in a right to consume subsistence quantities of meat and drink depends on his *labouring*. God gave the world to mankind in common, true, but more precisely, 'He gave it to the use of the Industrious and Rational, (and *Labour* was to be *his Title* to it;) not to the Fancy or Covetousness of the Quarrelsome and Contentious' (II, 34). In normal circumstances, no one has a direct right to meat and drink; everyone who is able-bodied must work for them. This point is affirmed particularly forcefully in the *First Treatise*.

> God sets him to work for his living, and seems rather to give him a Spade into his hand, to subdue the Earth, than a Scepter to Rule over its Inhabitants. In the Sweat of thy Face thou shalt eat thy Bread, says God to him, ver. 19. This was unavoidable, may it perhaps be answered, because he was yet without Subjects, and had no body to work for him, but afterwards . . . he might have People enough, whom he might command, to work for him; no, says God, not only whilst thou art without other help, save thy Wife, but as long as thou livest shall thou live by thy Labour. (I, 45)

This is not to deny, of course, that charity and inheritance also constitute titles to the means of preservation (I, 42). However, they are not, contrary to the traditional interpretation, generally available alternatives to labour. Rather, charity and inheritance apply *only* where a man is *unable* to labour.[53] If a man cannot labour, then obviously the use of the common does him no good and so he has a direct right to the surplusage of another's goods.

---

52. At least in the case of subsistence goods. We discuss the question of which specific rights are generated by Locke's argument in chapter 4 of this book.

53. This claim requires qualification in the case of inheritance. The only argument that Locke provides for inheritance concerns a right held by dependent children, as we

Charity for Locke is not due in virtue of need per se, but in virtue of need generated or made pressing by an inability to labour. Locke expressly so qualifies this right. 'Charity gives every Man a Title to so much out of another's Plenty, as will keep him from extream want, *where he has no means to subsist otherwise*' (I, 42; emphasis added). Since the ability to labour itself counts as a 'means to subsist,' need alone—in the simple sense of a lack of subsistence quantities of meat and drink—is insufficient for such a title.[54] Thus, if a man is in need, for whatever reason, yet is able to labour, then he has no right to be provided with consumption goods: 'I think that everyone, according to what way Providence has placed him in, is bound to labour for the publick good, as far as he is able, or else he has no right to eat.'[55] It is therefore at best misleading to refer, as is common practice, to the bearers of Locke's right of charity as the 'poor' or 'needy,' since this completely obscures the fact that there are needy individuals who do not enjoy any such right, namely, able-bodied ones.[56]

Similarly, the ground of the right of inheritance is also the inability to labour, obtaining here because of dependency. 'For Children being by the course of Nature, *born weak and unable to provide for themselves,*

---

discuss just below. With respect to that right, the claim in the text is simply correct. However, as we shall see in chapter 4, Locke also maintains, unargued, that non-dependent children have a right to inherit. Thus this right does not depend upon an inability to labour. Nevertheless, as we shall see at the end of this section, Locke also specifically holds that inheritance does not excuse one from labouring (if one is able) and so this right still does not constitute an *alternative* to labour.

54. A comparison with Lady Masham's account of Locke's own practice of charity is instructive here: '[Locke was] exceedingly charitable to those in want; but his charity was always directed to encourage working, laborious, industrious people, and not to relieve idle beggars, to whom he never gave anything, or would suffer his friends to do so before him, saying such people as those were "robbers of the poor," and asking those that went to relieve them "whether they knew none that were in want and deserved help;" if so, "how they could satisfy themselves to give anything they could spare to such as they *knew not to be in need*, but who probably deserved to be so?".' Emphasis added. Letter of Lady Masham to Jean LeClerc, 12 January, 1705, quoted in H. R. Fox Bourne, *The Life of John Locke*, vol. 2 (London: Henry S. King, 1876), pp. 535–36.

55. J. Locke, letter to William Molyneux, 19 January 1694, quoted in Tully, *DP*, p. 168.

56. Locke thought that the majority of needy individuals on public relief in his time fell into this category: 'For, upon a very modest computation, it may be concluded that above one half of those who receive relief from the parishes are able to get their livelihood.' Locke, *Report to the Board of Trade*, p. 378.

they have ... a Right to be nourished and maintained by their Parents' (I, 89, emphasis added; cf. II, 56, 79, 182–3). It is this right of maintenance which is the foundation of inheritance in Locke: 'the natural Right Children have to inherit the Goods of their Parents, being founded in the Right they have to the same Subsistence and Commodities of Life, out of the stock of their Parents' (I, 97; cf. I, 93). What makes the point most starkly here is Locke's strict insistence, even with children, on actual *inability* as the source of the right. For 'if it be necessary to his condition,' a father is free 'to make them work when they are able for their own Subsistence' (II, 64).

The conclusion that labour, to the extent that one is able, is the only legitimate way to exercise one's right to the means of preservation is precisely reflected in the structure of Locke's proposal for reforming the poor law. At the outset of his report, Locke categorises recipients of public relief with respect to their ability to labour for their own subsistence. Three categories are identified: 'First, those who can do nothing at all towards their own support. Secondly, those who, though they cannot maintain themselves wholly, yet are able to do something towards it. Thirdly, those who are able to maintain themselves by their own labour.'[57] Locke's proposals are geared towards compelling those in the second two categories to gain their subsistence, so far as possible, through their own labour rather than through public relief. Individuals in the third category would thereby be taken off public relief altogether, whereas those in the second category would continue to benefit from relief while nonetheless having to labour to the extent of their ability.[58] Children on relief, who belong to the second category, prove no exception; their attendance at working schools is made compulsory after the age of three.

It would be incorrect to suppose, however, that Locke's critical application of this labouring requirement was exclusively directed at the idle poor.[59] The requirement extends to all able-bodied individuals,

---

57. Locke, *Report to the Board of Trade*, p. 378.
58. 'But the greatest part of the poor maintained by parish rates are not absolutely unable nor wholly unwilling to do anything towards the getting of their livelihoods.... Their labour, therefore, as far as they are able to work, should be saved to the public.' Locke, *Report to the Board of Trade*, p. 382.
59. Hundert, 'Market Society and Meaning,' p. 39.

rich and poor alike.[60] Hence its implicit critique of idleness applies to idleness per se and can as well be directed at the idle rich.[61] That Locke did, in fact, so direct it is one of the conclusions for which Ashcraft argues, as we have seen,[62] in his *Revolutionary Politics*. This is the second of the two points on which Ashcraft's account of the practical context of Locke's argument supports my interpretation. Ironically, his conclusion there also undermines his own interpretation of Locke's right to the means of preservation presented in his other book, *Locke's Two Treatises of Government*.

Ashcraft's conclusion is that Locke's theory of property is intended in part as a radical critique of the idle element of the landowning aristocracy. This critique is said to stem from a 'socially rooted conception of labour and property' *(RP*, p. 266) that is highly critical of idleness, one whose locus in Locke's theory is that theory's identification of labour as the title to property (*RP*, pp. 262 and 257). But if that is so, then we cannot read that same theory as affirming a right to the means of preservation that is independent of one's labouring, for that would be to saddle the theory with what is tantamount to a licence for idleness. Thus Ashcraft's conclusion, if correct, supports my interpretation of this right.

Enough and as Good

One thing that remains curious on Waldron's interpretation is what the point might be of Locke's frequent (II, 31, 33–7) invocation of considerations of sufficiency, that is, his noting the existence of plenty after first qualifying his account of appropriation with it in II, 27. If, as Waldron

---

60. '[I]f those who are left by their predecessors a plentiful fortune are excused from having a particular calling in order to their subsistence in this life. 'Tis yet certain that by the law of God they are under an obligation of doing something.' Locke, 'Study,' MS. Locke, f. 2, pp. 101, 114. Quoted in Dunn, *Political Thought of John Locke*, p. 252n; cf. p. 231n.

61. Cf. Locke, *ELN*, fourth essay, f. 59, p. 157: 'Nor indeed can man believe . . . that all this equipment for action is bestowed on him by a most wise creator in order that he may do nothing, and that he is fitted out with all these faculties in order that he may thereby be more spendidly idle and sluggish.' See also, *ELN*, first essay, f. 18, p. 117.

62. See chapter 1, pp. 17–18, of this book.

contends, the fact that enough and as good has been left in common is *merely* a fact about appropriation in the age of abundance, why is it trumpeted so, and why in the manner of an assurance?

Locke introduces what we shall call the *sufficiency condition*—that an appropriation leaves enough and as good X for others[63]—in order to solve the consent problem. Recall that we have not as yet seen how this problem was solved. Satisfaction of the sufficiency condition explains why, in a context of original communism, the consent of each fellow commoner is not required to establish an individual property.

That this is the case also explains the manner in which appropriation is restricted by the sufficiency condition, for where this condition fails to obtain, consent cannot legitimately be forgone. Notice that this is different from saying that where it fails to obtain appropriation cannot proceed. Consensual appropriation is always legitimate (II, 38, 45, 50); it is not bound by the sufficiency condition. Hence, this condition does not bind absolutely and is therefore of a quite different order than the spoilage limitation. Indeed, it does not issue from natural law at all, but from the exigencies of the background context of original communism.

The key reason the consent of the other commoners is not required is set out in II, 33. Previously, it had been assumed that such consent was necessary because an appropriative act took something from the other commoners which belonged to them. Locke's strategy in circumventing this requirement is to argue that appropriation which satisfies the sufficiency condition does not take anything from the common at all and thus does not stand in need of the approval of other commoners: 'For he that leaves as much as another can make use of, does as good as take nothing at all' (II, 33). Since it is literally false that an appropriator who satisfies the sufficiency condition takes nothing at all, it is important to specify the respect in which Locke's appropriator does *as good as* take nothing at all. The point of reference here is given by the rights of the other commoners. Consent is not required because taking where enough and as good X is left for others is as good, so far as the rights of the other commoners are concerned, as taking nothing at all.

---

63. We designate that which is left in common in this way so as to leave it open for the moment whether it is left in kind.

Another way of putting Locke's point is that consent is not required because the acquisition of property subject to the stipulated condition does not *injure* the other commoners (II, 33), and so gives them no cause to complain. Again, their rights function as the point of reference. Appropriation subject to the sufficiency condition does not injure the other commoners because it does not violate their rights: 'it was impossible for any Man, this way, to intrench upon the right of another' (II, 36).

However the point is put, the rights in question are manifestly the commoners' rights to the means of preservation, that is, to property in common. This right, we have argued, is just the right not to be excluded from the use of the common materials from which the direct means of support can be produced. Appropriation transgresses this right whenever it vitiates the material preconditions of someone's exercise of it. These preconditions are vitiated wherever there are insufficient materials available for someone to produce subsistence quantities of meat, drink, and whatnot.

The sufficiency condition, it will be readily observed, serves precisely to ensure that the material preconditions of everyone's right to the means of preservation remain firmly in place. Satisfaction of this condition, then, prevents an appropriation from impinging on the other commoners' exercise of their right to property in common. Hence,

> he that had as good left for his Improvement, as was already taken up, needed not complain, ought not to meddle with what was already improved by another's Labour: If he did, 'tis plain he desired the benefit of another's Pains, which he had no right to, and not the Ground which God had given him in common with others to labour on, and whereof there was as good left, as that already possessed. (II, 34)

Labouring that satisfies the sufficiency condition is the nonconsensual method of individuating the common, the possibility of which was secured by Locke's paradox of plenty. It is legitimate because it respects the rights of the commoners and practical because it does not require universal consent.

Locke does, then, impose a sufficiency condition on natural appropriation. The question thus focuses on whether this condition is consistent with scarcity of land. This narrower issue may be prosecuted by asking whether that which is left in common for others need be left in kind. Natural appropriation of land is certainly legitimate where enough and as good *land* is left in common for others,[64] in keeping with the first part of Waldron's expansion.[65] What remains to be seen is whether there is anything else that—if enough and as good of it were left—would also satisfy the sufficiency condition.

Tully and Community Ownership

In *A Discourse on Property*, Tully denies that anything besides land itself can satisfy the sufficiency condition. This conclusion is predicated on the claim that, where all the land is under cultivation, 'others are excluded from exercising their natural claim right' (p. 152).[66] Hence, when 'land becomes scarce and men's claim rights conflict, then the theory of natural appropriation and use has no application' (p. 165). The conclusion Tully then draws is that all exclusive rights in that land are void: 'goods once legitimately acquired can no longer be retained in exclusive possession, but revert to common ownership' (p. 165). Some new method of individuation is thus required so that men may exercise their right to the means of preservation. This new method is civil law.

Tully's radical suggestion that 'community ownership of all possessions is the logical consequence of Locke's theory in the *Two Treatises*' (p. 165) is therefore integrally related to the contention that what the sufficiency condition requires to be left in common for others must be left for them in kind. If this were not the case, the natural property regime would still be legitimate under conditions of scarcity and there would be no need for individuation based on consent.

---

64. The ambiguity noted earlier as to whether the basis of comparison is the initial communal holding or the newly appropriated individual one is actually difficult to adjudicate by the text alone. II, 34 clearly supports the latter reading, while II, 35 explicitly supports the former. The logic of the argument, however, requires the former reading. For what the sufficiency condition ensures is that any given appropriation does not encroach on the other commoners' exercise of their right to the means of preservation. On the latter reading, the condition is plainly too weak to perform this function.

65. It is a further weakness of Waldron's own interpretation that it provides no explanation of whence the certainty of an appropriation's legitimacy in this case obtains.

66. Cf. Cohen, *Marx and Locke*, pp. 379–81.

The ground of this contention is the supposition that scarcity of land excludes the claim-rights of some men. Because the sufficiency condition is meant to safeguard these rights, supposing this much entails that the condition must act to forestall such scarcity, that is, to ensure that enough and as good *land* is left in common. However, this supposition obtains only in virtue of the implicit presupposition that men have a natural right to land (or, what is the same thing, that property in land is a necessary condition of the exercise of some natural right). At the heart of this interpretation of the sufficiency condition, therefore, is the understanding that men have a natural right to land in Locke.

It is curious that Tully would employ such an understanding in arriving at one of his central claims, since he specifically denies that there is a natural right to land.

> A property in something is the completion of man's natural right to the means necessary to preserve and comfort himself and others. It is a paramount and remarkable feature of this initial claim right that it is not to the earth itself, but to the manmade products useful to man's life. (p. 122)

Nevertheless, noting this inconsistency is inadequate as a repudiation of the putative natural right to land because the inconsistency can only be generated by embracing an erroneous interpretation of the right to the means of preservation.

On the present interpretation, the natural right safeguarded by the sufficiency condition is the right to the means of preservation. It discharges this function by securing the material preconditions of this right, the right to produce subsistence quantities of meat, drink, and whatnot. More precisely, the right is an inclusive right of access to the common materials that God provided for the purpose of actualising—in consumption, but through labour—the prior right to preserve oneself (I, 87).

Having property in land is simply not a necessary precondition of the exercise of this right. Certainly, for the able-bodied, it is a sufficient, and arguably the most desirable, manner of exercising one's right to the means of preservation, but it is not the only one. For it is equally true that for Locke labouring on someone else's property for payment which is, or enables one to purchase, the means of subsistence and comfort also exercises this same right.

This conclusion is similar to a part of Macpherson's view[67] and might therefore seem to involve the difficulties associated with the servant/wage-labourer debate.[68] However, there are two distinct aspects of this debate, as indeed there are of Macpherson's position here, only one of which bears on the present argument. Its principal aspect is the controversial question of whether servants in Locke are proto-proletarians who sell their *labour-power* for a wage to proto-capitalist landlords, or whether the labour which servants sell to masters is rather a complete task or service performed under their own direction. Quite separate from this is the subsidiary question of whether, in Locke, one may be driven by the absence of unappropriated land to sell one's labour, however conceived, to a landlord—that is, to be compelled to become a servant—or whether instead 'since it is a freeman who makes himself a servant, the agreement must presuppose that the choice not to become a servant is available to him' (p. 137). It is only this subsidiary aspect of the debate which affects the point at hand.

What is certain is that Locke allowed both that one man might properly become the servant of another (II, 77, 85) and that it could come to pass that all the land in some part of the world is possessed (II, 184; cf. II, 45). What is as yet uncertain is whether both of these situations may coexist (that is, whether the legitimacy of the existence of one situation requires the nonexistence of the other). Tully's conclusion that they may not is based on three considerations.

First, he interprets I, 42 as implying that if one is driven by necessity to work for another, then the relation is based on force and is, ipso facto, a master and vassal arrangement—and hence illegitimate (p. 137).

> [A] Man can no more justly make use of another's necessity, to force him to become his Vassal, by with-holding that Relief, God requires him to afford to the wants of his Brother, than he that has more strength can seize upon a weaker, master him to his Obedience, and with a Dagger at his Throat offer him Death or Slavery. (I, 42)

---

67. C. B. Macpherson, *The Political Theory of Possessive Individualism* (Oxford: Clarendon Press, 1962), pp. 213–14.
68. See P. Laslett, 'Market Society and Political Theory,' *Historical Journal* 7 (1) (1964), pp. 150–54; Macpherson, *Political Theory of Possessive Individualism*, pp. 215 ff.; C. B. Macpherson, *Democratic Theory: Essays in Retrieval* (Oxford: Clarendon Press, 1973), essay 12; Tully, *DP*, pp. 135–45; J. Waldron, 'The Turfs My Servant Has Cut,' *Locke Newsletter* 13 (1982), pp. 9–20.

Yet, as Waldron has also pointed out,[69] Locke carefully distinguishes the power that a master has over a servant from that which he has over a slave or vassal (II, 2), and therefore the fact that one may not be driven by necessity into the latter relation does not imply that one may not be so driven into the former.

Second, Tully argues that, strictly speaking, necessity arising from landlessness naturally realises a man's right to subsistence in the surplus goods of another, rather than compelling a man into another's service: 'A person is not allowed to treat another in this way; he must feed him instead' (p. 137). Here Tully's argument clearly turns on the mistaken reading of the right to the means of preservation and thus cannot be upheld. It is only the necessity arising from an incapacity to labour that underpins the right of charity.

Finally, Tully invokes II, 85, in which servants are contrasted with slaves, the essence of slavery being propertylessness. However, Locke is plainly using 'property' in his extended sense here, as he characterises slaves as having 'forfeited their Lives, and with it their Liberties, and lost their Estates' (II, 85; cf. II, 173–4), and so nothing of immediate relevance follows from this particular contrast.

There is, in short, no good reason to suppose that Locke held that exercising one's right to the means of preservation by labouring on another's land requires, as a condition of its legitimacy, that unappropriated land be available as an alternative. It follows, then, that labouring on another's land itself independently constitutes a legitimate means of exercising this natural right. This, in turn, is sufficient to establish that property in land is not a necessary condition of exercising the right to the means of preservation. There is therefore no natural right to land in Locke.

The salient differences between those who exercise their right to produce subsistence quantities of meat, drink, and whatnot through property in land (which obtains in virtue of their having laboured on previously common land or having inherited it, ultimately, from those who did) and those who do so by labouring on the land of this first group will be, first, the actual possession of the land and, second, a (doubtless) differential abundance of goods beyond the level needed for comfort and

---

69. Waldron, 'Turfs My Servant Has Cut,' p. 13.

support. To neither of these does anyone have a prior natural right. Scarcity of land under these conditions thus excludes the rights of no one.

In passing, it is worth noting that the ground of Tully's claim that community ownership of all possessions is the logical consequence of the premisses of Locke's theory has been undermined. For without first invalidating the natural property regime, there is no way even to set the stage for community ownership. Tully's designated mechanism, the advent of land scarcity, fails, however, to perform this task.

Labour's Abundance

The sufficiency condition is consistent with scarcity of land because that scarcity does not per se imperil any of the rights which the condition is intended to safeguard. Naturally, there are contexts in which scarcity of land would do just that. To begin with, if those without land were denied the opportunity to labour on someone else's land, then clearly they would be prevented from exercising their natural rights and in that degree would be injured. Hence, under conditions of scarcity, there attaches to property in land, as a condition of its continuing legitimacy, the obligation to employ those without land of their own.[70] As we have said, no one may be denied access to the materials necessary to produce the direct means of subsistence. This is a matter of natural right.

Furthermore, if the land once appropriated were less able to sustain people labouring on it than when it lay in common, then there would also be people who were prevented from exercising their natural rights and who would be in that degree injured by that appropriation. That is, if the number of people who could be preserved by labouring on a given plot of land lying in common were greater than the number who could be so preserved subsequent to that plot's appropriation, then, under conditions of scarcity, the appropriation in question would injure those people who could no longer be preserved.

---

70. This obligation may also be discharged by simply handing over the means of subsistence. Notice that this obligation obtains in virtue of the sufficiency condition and is independent of that of charity, which obtains over the set of disabled (as opposed to landless) individuals.

Hence, for the sufficiency condition to be satisfied, appropriated land must be able to sustain at least as many people as it was capable of sustaining while held in common. This is just to say that appropriation is only legitimate where *enough and as good direct means of subsistence are available for others*.[71] In ensuring this much, the sufficiency condition discharges its task of securing the material preconditions of the right to the means of preservation. It will thus be observed that what must be left for others need not be left in kind.

Now it is an integral part of Locke's theory of property that natural appropriation by labour satisfies this condition. Locke argues for this in a much misunderstood part of chapter 5, namely II, 40–43 (Olivecrona's 'part B').[72] These paragraphs are explicitly advanced in order to establish that the 'Products of the Earth useful to the Life of Man' produced on land appropriated by labour overbalance those produced on common land: 'Nor is it so strange, as perhaps before consideration it may appear, that the Property of labour should be able to over-ballance the Community of Land' (II, 40).

Locke argues that the abundance of labour is manifested by the contrast of America (where land lies in common) with England (where the land has been cultivated, and thus appropriated, by labour): 'a King of a large and fruitful Territory there feeds, lodges and is clad worse than a day Labourer in England' (II, 41). The comparison needs to be made with uncultivated rather than with cultivated common land because cultivation of common land appropriates it, ipso facto (II, 34, 45).

This same conclusion is secured more generally by Locke's claim that 'labour makes the far greatest part of the value of things, we enjoy in this World' (II, 42). This claim has traditionally been read as distinct from the main line of Locke's argument in chapter 5 and as forming what is sometimes called his labour theory of value.[73]

I submit, however, that the value-creation language is principally a shorthand enabling labour's de novo creation—the amount it adds to the

---

71. It remains the case, however, that these others will have to labour in order to produce or even simply to acquire their direct means of subsistence.

72. Cf. Buckle, *Natural Law*, pp. 158–59.

73. See Olivecrona, 'Locke's Theory of Appropriation,' pp. 231–34; Cohen, *Marx and Locke*, pp. 369–70; Waldron, 'Enough and as Good,' p. 324.

common stock beyond the contribution of nature—to be factored out and thus appreciated. Since the original natural materials had some use (value) in their common state,[74] the complete product does not represent labour's contribution to the common stock. The value-added language captures precisely what labour does in fact contribute.

On Locke's accounting, ninety-nine percent of the available direct means of subsistence are the products of labour (II, 40) and have thus been added by appropriation to the common stock. It follows that appropriated land can sustain many more people than it could have done while lying in common, or that appropriation leaves much more than enough and as good for others—ninety-nine times more, in fact.

This reading is strengthened immeasurably by considering the marginal addition which Locke made to II, 37 (perhaps in order to clarify his original, somewhat obscure point). In this addition, which, significantly, follows immediately on a restatement of the sufficiency condition,[75] Locke makes exactly the argument given in II, 40–43:

> To which let me add, that he who appropriates land to himself by his labour, does not lessen but increase the common stock of mankind. For the provisions serving to the support of humane life, produced by one acre of inclosed and cultivated land, are (to speak much within compass) ten times more, than those, which are yielded by an acre of land, of an equal richnesse, lyeing wast in common. (II, 37)

He even employs practically the same figures as in II, 40 to quantify labour's abundance[76] and again equates the productivity of cultivated English land and one hundred times as much wild American land.

---

74. The course of argument in II, 41–43 also reinforces the interpretation that what was originally provided in common by God was the materials necessary to produce the means of preservation. 'Nature and the Earth furnished only the almost worthless Materials, as in themselves' (II, 43).

75. 'Yet this could not be much, nor to the Prejudice of others, where the same plenty was still left, to those who would use the same Industry. To which let me add . . .' (II, 37). The addition thus clearly explicates the sufficiency condition and in a fashion which ties it closely to the reading of II, 40–43 argued for here.

76. Here ten times, later changed to one hundred; there nine times, later changed to ninety-nine times, but expressed as 9/10 and 99/100, which are easily confused for the II, 37 figures.

Both Cohen and Waldron dissent from this reading of II, 37.[77] They suggest that the benefit of labour's abundance lies not in the surplus product of the appropriated acres of land, but in the reduced pressure on the remaining ninety. However, the text of II, 37 itself is ambiguous on this point, for Locke does not specify whether the increase in the common stock occasioned by labour is a per capita increase or a gross increase. By contrast, Locke makes explicit use of the present reading in II, 36 with regard to Spain, where 'the Inhabitants think themselves beholden to him, who, by his Industry on neglected, and consequently waste Land, has increased the stock of Corn, which they wanted.'

Reading II, 40–43 as an argument that natural appropriation satisfies the sufficiency condition has the further merit of making sense of the continuity of Locke's text.[78] The first sentence of II, 40 indicates that what follows is part of a continuous argument, as that of II, 44 does for what preceded it: 'From all of which it is evident, that though the things of Nature are given in common, yet Man ... had still in himself the great Foundation of Property.'[79] Even Olivecrona has trouble accounting for this 'still.'[80]

It is true that, on Locke's argument, natural appropriation satisfies the sufficiency condition almost necessarily. Nevertheless, the significance of this condition should not therefore be discounted. In the context of Locke's theory of property, it is just because this sufficiency condition is satisfied that natural appropriation is legitimate notwithstanding the

77. Cohen, *Marx and Locke*, p. 380; Waldron, 'Enough and as Good,' p. 323, and *RPP*, p. 170.
78. Waldron, 'Enough and as Good,' p. 324n., writes that both II, 37 and 40–43 are 'widely regarded as insertions.' While lines 10–32 of II, 37 do represent a marginal addition (as we have said), in II, 40–43 only lines 24–32 of II, 42 (which are irrelevant here) represent a later addition. See Laslett, collation to *Two Treatises of Government*. The only authority for regarding II, 40–43 as an insertion is Olivecrona's suggestion to that effect ('Locke's Theory of Appropriation,' pp. 233–34), which Waldron cites. But his suggestion turns on misunderstanding the point of these paragraphs as a discussion of value distinct from the main thread of Locke's argument. Only then does this section 'not fit well into the context.'
79. This Cohen concedes at p. 369n, *Marx and Locke*. This air of continuity is put down to confusion on Locke's part.
80. Olivecrona, 'Locke's Theory of Appropriation,' p. 233.

absence of universal consent.[81] What is more, an argument was required to establish that it is in fact satisfied. That it turns out almost always to be satisfied is to the credit of Locke's argument.

---

81. It follows, contrary to the traditional interpretation, that there is no argument in Locke (because there is no room for one) establishing the manner in which the sufficiency condition is circumvented.

3

Mixing or Making?

Locke's argument for the legitimacy of private property is a single argument with two interdependent parts. One part of the argument aims to explain why appropriation, even in a context of original communism, does not require anyone else's consent. As we have seen, Locke's answer is that consent is not required because appropriation does not violate anyone's rights as long as sufficient materials are effectively available for everyone to produce his subsistence. Locke's stipulation of the sufficiency condition is meant to guarantee that these materials are always available and so that consent is never required.

Given that no one's consent is required, the other part of the argument aims to explain what makes the appropriation of particular things legitimate. Locke's answer is that the appropriation of things is legitimated by one's labouring on them. But on its own, of course, this leaves it unexplained *why* it is that labour legitimates appropriation. The traditional interpretation, as we have seen, has Locke taking property in one's person and labour for granted and arguing from there that labour legitimates appropriation because, in labouring, one irretrievably mixes with the object something that one already owns, namely, one's labour. In this chapter, I shall present and defend an alternative interpretation of Locke's explanation of labour's legitimating power, beginning with some criticism of the traditional interpretation.

Labour, Mixing, and the Tradition

As an *argument*, the traditional construction suffers from a number of serious and well-known flaws.[1] The most important of these is perhaps the fact that its crucial inference is simply a non sequitur. This is the point famously made by Nozick's example of pouring a tin of tomato juice that one owns into the sea: 'Why isn't mixing what I own with what I don't a way of losing what I own rather than a way of gaining what I don't?' (*ASU*, p. 174–75). Certainly, in this case, the conclusion would be that one had foolishly lost the tomato juice.

It has sometimes been suggested that Nozick's criticism can be mitigated by locating the mixture argument properly in Locke's natural law framework.[2] On this suggestion, the mixture argument is not to be regarded as a complete argument in itself, but rather as a completion of an earlier argument in chapter 5. We are thus to distinguish two stages of Locke's argument. In the first stage, Locke argues that individual property rights are legitimate on the ground that appropriation of items from the common is necessary if the common is to be useful for the preservation of mankind, as God intended.[3] In the second stage, Locke demonstrates how one may come to own particular things. It is only at this point that recourse to the mixture argument is supposed to be made.[4]

This response, however, is manifestly inadequate. For even if we accept the two-stage analysis, and hence that the mixture argument is meant to function in the context of a prior demonstration of the legitimacy of individual property rights, we are not thereby licensed to make

---

1. Interestingly, it does not suffer from one flaw commonly attributed to it, namely, that 'mixing' yields impossible results when iterated with the same object over different agents. See Miller, 'Justice and Property,' pp. 6–7. Locke clearly stipulates that labouring only gives rise to a property where it is applied to objects that are in 'the State that Nature hath provided and left' (II, 27; cf. II, 32, lines 7–8, 11–12, 15–17, 19–20).

2. See, e.g., D. C. Snyder, 'Locke on Natural Law and Property Rights,' *Canadian Journal of Philosophy* 16 (4) (1986), pp. 733–38.

3. 'His argument [II, 26] is that since God has given the earth to man for his support and comfort he means for man to use it. But to use most things an individual must appropriate them. In other words, preservation demands that persons use objects, but to use them they must first appropriate them, must own them.' Snyder, 'Locke on Natural Law,' p. 735.

4. Snyder, 'Locke on Natural Law,' pp. 734–35.

the inference criticised by Nozick.[5] Of course, accepting that analysis does mean that less hangs on the non sequitur, and so, in that sense, the criticism could be mitigated by doing so. But this merely relocates the inadequacy, since the two-stage analysis is itself marred by its dependence on a misinterpretation of II, 26. As we have already argued, the point of Locke's paradox of plenty—of which II, 26 forms a part—is not to legitimate individual property rights, but rather to refute the assumption that universal consent is the unique sufficient condition of legitimate appropriation. Hence there is no earlier argument for this conclusion the mixture argument can be seen as completing.

Another serious flaw is found in the axiomatic status attributed to the property that Locke affirms in one's person and in one's labour. These properties merit this status only if their inherence is self-evident, or at the very least distinctly more obvious than the conclusion to be drawn. Yet the self-evidence of these premisses appears to rest on some suspect logical equivocation. Alan Ryan has put the point well:

> It is a very dangerous way of talking, for it swiftly confuses the 'his' of identification with the 'his' of ownership or rightful possession. Thus, there is a perfectly good sense in which: 'The Labour of his Body, and the Work of his Hands, we may say, are properly his' (II, 27). But this sense needs elucidating. In one sense it is bound to be 'his,' as it is a truth of logic that only *he* can do *his* labouring, and in this sense, whomever he labours for, it is still 'his' labour. But this does not establish that the only person entitled to benefit from his labour is himself.[6]

Plainly, we need not impute some such equivocation to the argument, but if we do not, it is then doubtful whether these premisses are as obvious as their status requires.

---

5. Either the general background fact that individual property rights are legitimate itself entitles one to appropriate a given item from the common, X, or it does not. If it does, then the mixture argument is superfluous. If it does not, then it remains mysterious why one would not simply forfeit one's labour in mixing it with X. In neither case has it been shown that ownership of X follows *from* the fact that one owned the labour that one had mixed with X.

6. Ryan, 'Locke and the Dictatorship of the Bourgeoisie,' p. 225; cf. J. P. Day, 'Locke on Property,' *Philosophical Quarterly* 16 (1966), pp. 207–21; Held, 'John Locke on Robert Nozick,' p. 181.

As *interpretation*, the traditional view, though heavy-handed, has the merit of straightforward congruence with much of the text. Consequently, one typically has the impression that Locke's theory, when scrutinised, is not very compelling. Sometimes an attempt is made to shore up the argument by reconstructing it in terms of, say, value creation or desert.[7] What never seems to be questioned is the assumption that these various flaws, their gravity notwithstanding, exhibit weaknesses in Locke's argument rather than in the traditional *interpretation* of that argument.

The Workmanship Model

A superior interpretation of the metaphorical labour mixture theme in Locke's argument is the one drawn by James Tully. On his interpretation, the central ground of Locke's theory of property is a relational model 'of God as maker and man as his workmanship' (*DP*, p. 4), which Tully calls the *workmanship model*. The crucial feature of this model is its supposition, which 'is clearly taken to be self-evident and undeniable,' that 'a maker has a right in and over his workmanship' (*DP*, p. 42). Now, for Locke, a right is, in general, equivalent to a property: 'the idea of property being a right to anything.'[8] Hence, what a maker is said to have is a property in his workmanship. We shall call this *the doctrine of maker's right*.

Locke explicitly affirms this doctrine when he first introduces his common-sense premiss in the *Second Treatise* in order to explain God's property in man:[9]

---

7. Value creation: Nozick, *ASU*, p. 175. Nozick does not himself endorse this gloss. Desert: Miller, 'Justice and Property,' pp. 6–7.

8. J. Locke, *An Essay Concerning Human Understanding*, ed. P. H. Nidditch (Oxford: Clarendon Press, 1975), bk. IV, chap. iii, sec. 18. All subsequent references to this work are simply by book, chapter, and section number. For a detailed defence of the practice of using the *Essay* to facilitate the interpretation of the *Two Treatises*, see Tully, *DP*, pp. 5–8.

9. The explanation of the binding authority of natural law which we gave in chapter 2 should, strictly speaking, be put in terms of man's being God's property, that is, in terms of the right which God *qua* maker has in man and the corresponding obligation which man has *qua* workmanship. It will thus be observed that the doctrine of maker's right underpins not only Locke's labour theory of property, but also the framework of natural law and natural rights within which it is articulated.

Mixing or Making? 63

> For Men being all the Workmanship of one Omnipotent, and infinitely wise Maker; All the Servants of one Sovereign Master, sent into the World on his order and about his business, *they are his Property, whose Workmanship they are*, made to last during his, not one anothers pleasure. (II, 6; emphasis added)

The thrust of the workmanship interpretation is that, in Tully's words,

> due to the analogy between God and man as makers, anything true of one will be, *ceteris paribus*, true of the other. Since [the doctrine of maker's right] is the explanation of God's dominion over man and of why man is God's 'property,' it also explains man's dominion over and property in the products of his making. (*DP*, p. 37)

Notice that the logical structure of the *analogy* is such that its conclusion—namely, that men are entitled to a property in the products of their making—actually holds independently of the existence of God,[10] although Tully appears to suggest otherwise (*DP*, pp. 35ff.). This is because its point of departure takes the form of a conditional—if God makes something, then He is entitled to a property in it—while the comparison it advances is simply that men's making is sufficiently God-like, that is, like the sort of making envisaged in the foregoing antecedent, that a similar conditional applies to men. Locke, of course, believed that the antecedent of the original conditional did in fact obtain.[11] But the force of his conclusion that a similar conditional, namely, the maker's right doctrine, applies by analogy to men's making does not require the truth of this belief.

In order fully to understand the basis of this analogy, we will need to follow Tully in making reference to some features of Locke's concept of *making*, as drawn from the analysis of the *Essay*. Making, in Locke's technical sense, belongs to one of two sorts of cause. A *cause* is 'that which makes any other thing . . . begin to be' (II.xxvi.2). The first sort of cause holds 'when the thing is wholly made new, so that no part thereof did ever exist before; . . . and this we call *creation*' (II.xxvi.2). The second sort of cause holds 'when a thing is made up of particles, which did

---

10. I am grateful to Jerry Cohen for emphasising to me the importance of clarifying this point.
11. His invocation of the maker's right doctrine to explain *God's* property in man—as opposed to man's property in his workmanship—obviously does presuppose that God exists, but that is already presupposed by the *explanandum*.

all of them before exist; but that very thing, so constituted of pre-existing particles, which, considered all together, make up such a collection of simple ideas, had not any existence before' (II.xxvi.2). Locke distinguishes three causes of this second sort; in particular, 'when the cause is extrinsical, and the effect produced by a sensible separation, or juxta position of discernible parts, we call it *making*; and such are all artificial things' (II.xxvi.2).[12] This is the technical definition of making.

It will be convenient, however, to recognise for the moment that, in addition to this technical sense, there is a broader sense of 'making' applicable here, one which comprises both making, strictly so-called, and creation. For creation can readily be seen as simply 'making ex nihilo.' Making some thing may thus be understood loosely in the general causal sense of bringing that thing into being, if we disregard the question, *Ex quo*? This is not to suggest that the strict distinction between creation and making is of no consequence. Indeed, we shall elaborate its significance later. Nevertheless, since we shall also see that the maker's right doctrine embraces both creation and making, it will be useful to have recourse to a single, comprehensive term.

The activity of making, on Locke's analysis, is governed by the *idea* of that thing which the maker thereby brings into being. A maker, that is, effects the material realisation of some idea of his, one which constitutes the essence of the thing made: 'the idea or essence of the several sorts of artificial things, consisting for the most part in nothing but the determinate figure of sensible parts, and sometimes motion depending thereon, which the artificer fashions in matter, such as he finds for his turn' (III.vi.40). It follows, then, as Tully states, that 'there is an analytic relationship between being a maker and knowing the description [idea] under which what is made is made' (*DP*, p. 36). For, as Locke puts it, 'an artificial thing [is] a production of man, which the artificer designed, and therefore well knows the idea of' (III.vi.40).[13]

---

12. The other two causes are 'generation' and 'alteration' (II.xxvi.2).

13. Compare: 'had we such a knowledge of that constitution of man, from which his faculties of moving, sensation, and reasoning, and other powers flow, and on which his so regular shape depends, as it is possible angels have, and it is certain his Maker has, we should have a quite other idea of his essence than what is now contained in our definition of that species' (III.vi.3).

The salient conclusion which emerges from this discussion is that making is an activity with an essentially intellectual dimension. Anyone who is not an intellectual being, therefore, is incapable of making anything. The importance of this conclusion to the workmanship interpretation makes itself manifest in Locke's claim in the *Two Treatises* that it is precisely in respect of his similarity to God *qua* intellectual creature that man is capable of dominion, that is, property: 'God makes him in his own Image after his own Likeness, makes him an intellectual Creature, and so capable of Dominion' (I, 30; cf. I, 40).[14] It is clear, then, that man owes his capacity to own property to his intellectual nature.

Now, the fact that man's capacity for making something and his capacity for owning something both depend on his intellectual nature does not itself entail that his ownership of property is founded on the maker's right doctrine. However, as we have seen, God's property does arise as a consequence of His making (II, 6; I, 53). Therefore, since man's capacity for owning property obtains in virtue of his similarity to God, it would seem reasonable to infer that man's property arises likewise as a consequence of his making.

What strengthens the grounds for this conclusion immeasurably is the fact that postulating the maker's right doctrine enables us to explain exactly why it is that man owes his capacity for property to his *intellectual* similarity to God. The explanation is this. Given that it is the activity of making which gives rise to property, then since it is a requirement of being able to make anything that one has an intellectual nature, it follows that anyone who lacked an intellectual nature would be incapable of owning property.

We turn now to an elucidation of the manner in which the doctrine of maker's right underpins the property rights which Locke asserts in II, 27—namely, the property which men have in their own persons and labour and which they may come to have in distinct parts of the common. To begin with, it may be wondered how it is possible for man at once to be God's property and to have a property in his own person and

---

14. Lest it be doubted that it is specifically man's intellectual nature which is the basis of his capacity for dominion, the text continues: 'For wherein soever else the Image of God consisted, the intellectual Nature was certainly a part of it, and belong'd to the whole Species, and enabled them to have Dominion' (I, 30).

labour. The appearance of difficulty here, however, is easily dissolved. In the *Essay*, Locke clearly distinguishes between *man* and *person*: 'But whatever to some men makes a man, and consequently the same individual man, wherein perhaps few are agreed, personal identity can by us be placed in nothing but consciousness, (which is that alone which makes what we call self)' (II.xxvii.21). Locke elaborates further upon this distinction in his replies to John Sergeant's critique of the *Essay*: 'A man has the individuality of a man before he has Knowledg but is not a person before he has Knowledg.' Hence, 'person,' in contradistinction to 'man,' 'is the name for a unity which is not first given and then known, but rather exists only by virtue of its being constituted by consciousness.'[15] If we now read the text of II, 27 with this distinction in mind, we shall see that, as Tully has pointed out (*DP*, p. 108), Locke carefully writes that 'every Man has a *Property* in his own *Person*. . . . The *Labour* of his Body, and the *Work* of his Hands, we may say, are properly his' (II, 27).[16] What God enjoys, therefore, is a property in man, whereas what man enjoys is a property in his own person and labour.[17]

God's property, as we have said, obtains because He made man. In order for man's property to arise on a similar basis, it must be the case that man makes his own person and labour. The sense in which this is in fact so has been well brought out by Tully (*DP*, pp. 106–8). *Person*, as Locke defines it, 'is a Forensick Term, appropriating actions and their merit; and so belongs only to intelligent agents, capable of a law, and happiness, and misery' (II.xxvii.26). Personality is thus implicitly re-

---

15. This quotation and the previous one are taken from U. Thiel, 'Locke's Concept of Person,' in *John Locke: Symposium Wolfenbüttel 1979*, ed. R. Brandt (Berlin: Walter de Gruyter, 1981), pp. 184–85. Locke's replies to Sergeant are contained in some marginal notes in Locke's copy of Sergeant's *Solid Philosophy Asserted, Against the Fancies of the Ideists: Or, The Method to Science Farther Illustrated. With Reflections on Mr. Locke's Essay concerning Human Understanding*, London, 1697.

16. Contrast Grotius: 'A Man's life is his own by Nature . . . and so is his Body, his Limbs, his Reputation, his Honour, and his Actions.' *De Iure Belli ac Pacis*, 1625, 1.17.2.1. Quoted in Tully, *DP*, p. 80. Contrast also Richard Baxter: 'Every man is born with a propriety in his *own members*.' *The Second Part of the Nonconformists Plea for Peace*, London, 1680, p. 54. Quoted in Laslett, ed. note to II, 27, *Two Treatises of Government*, p. 329.

17. Cf. Tully, *DP*, p. 109: 'His body and his limbs are God's property: the actions he uses them to make are his own.'

stricted to free agents, since freedom is a condition of the capacity for law (I.iii.14; cf. II, 57).

Freedom, on Locke's analysis, 'consists in the dependence of the Existence, or not Existence of any Action, upon our volition of it' (II.xxi.27), where volition in turn 'is an act of the Mind directing its thought to the production of any Action [or forbearance thereof], and thereby exerting its power to produce it' (II.xxi.28). Actions, therefore, are brought into existence according to the volition of free agents. Moreover, they are each brought into existence under a particular idea which fixes the criterion of their identity. That this is the case emerges from Locke's discussion of personal identity. There he argues, inter alia, that 'as far as this consciousness can be extended backwards to any past Action or Thought, so far reaches the Identity of that Person' (II.xxvii.9). In explicating this claim, Locke makes it clear that it is specifically insofar as it 'can repeat the Idea of any past Action with the same consciousness it had of it at first, and with the same consciousness it has of any present Action' that an intelligent Being constitutes 'the same personal self' (II.xxvii.10).

But if an action is brought into existence by a free, intelligent agent under an idea which determines the identity of that action, this is just to say that the action is *made* by the agent; for that, as we have seen, is what making is. Thus it follows, on the maker's right doctrine, that the agent owns that action; that it is her property. This conclusion Locke upholds at several places in the *Essay*, most notably as follows:

> That with which the consciousness of this present thinking thing can join itself, makes the same Person, and is one self with it, and with nothing else; and so attributes to it self, and owns all the Actions of that thing, as its own, as far as that consciousness reaches, and no farther. (II.xxvii.17; cf. 24, 26)

As Tully puts it, 'the criterion of ownership is consciousness of having performed those actions, of being their author' (*DP*, 108).

In the *Two Treatises*, of course, what Locke actually says is that every man has a property in his *labour*. Nevertheless, in this context Locke plainly takes 'labour' and 'action' to be interchangeable; for example, he writes in II, 44, 'by being Master of himself, and Proprietor of his own Person and the actions or Labour of it.' The maker's right doctrine, then, underlies property in labour in a relatively straightforward manner.

It is rather more difficult to make out a strict sense in which a man makes his person. It is true that all of a man's thoughts and actions, the unification of which by consciousness constitutes his person, are made by him and so are his property. But this does not establish that a man's person itself is made by him, though it does (importantly) preclude someone else's having made his person—'someone else' being any man other than the one who made the thoughts and actions comprised by the person in question. That said, it should also be recognised that it is property in labour which is the significant case. Property in one's person is not integral to the force of the argument because property in labour is derived independently of it. Hence, it is not such a grave problem that a man's person may be his in no more than the truistic sense of the 'his' of identification.

There remains the central and most important case of the property that men may come to have in distinct parts of the common. On the workmanship model, the right a man enjoys in the product of his labour arises from his having made that product from the common materials provided by God. What man's labouring on the common makes are useful goods and the conveniences of life. As Locke remarks in his journal of 1677, 'Nature furnishes us only with the material, for the most part rough and unfitted to our use; it requires labour, art, and thought, to suit them to our occasions.'[18] Thus, to take as our example 'the chief matter of Property' (II, 32), a field ploughed in virgin territory is a useful product that is newly made by man from the ground, which 'is called, as indeed it is, wast' (II, 42), through the labour of tilling, cultivating, and so on. In this cultivated field man accordingly acquires a maker's right, that is, a property. 'As much Land as a Man Tills, Plants, Improves, Cultivates, and can use the Product of, so much is his Property. He by his Labour does, as it were, inclose it from the Common' (II, 32).

This, then, is the alternative interpretation of the labour mixture theme that lies at the heart of Locke's explanation of individual property in the *Two Treatises*. Although some evidence in its favour has already been adduced, we have so far been primarily concerned to articulate clearly the content of this interpretation and to establish its application to the

---

18. MS. Locke, f. 2, fos. 247–55. Quoted in Tully, *DP*, p. 121; cf. II, 40–43.

various property rights in question. We are now in a position to consider the preponderance of evidence for upholding the workmanship interpretation over the traditional one.

God and Creation

The primary occasion for the invocation of the maker's right doctrine in Locke's theory is the explanation of the property God enjoys in all Creation. We have already seen that Locke clearly makes recourse to this doctrine right at the outset of the *Second Treatise* to account for God's ownership of man in particular (II, 6). To this may be added the equally straightforward testimony of the *First Treatise*: 'he has so visible a claim to us as his Workmanship, that one of the ordinary Apellations of God in Scripture is, God our Maker and the Lord our Maker.... [F]or he is King because he is indeed Maker of us all' (I, 53). Locke's reliance on the maker's right doctrine on this point, however, is far from confined to these passages in the *Two Treatises*. In fact, the doctrine is one he asserts in some of his earliest writings, the *Essays on the Law of Nature*, and which he continues to hold in the *Essay* as well.[19] As we shall see, quite apart from its function in Locke's theory of property, the doctrine of maker's right constitutes an integral element not only of his analysis of natural law but also of his grounds for believing in the possibility of a demonstrative science of morality. Hence there is but little exaggeration in Tully's claim that 'the workmanship model is a fundamental feature of all Locke's writings' (*DP*, p. 4).

It will be apposite to recall here that what we have called the doctrine of maker's right is formulated in terms of 'making' in the broad sense, that is, one which comprises both creating and making, strictly so-called.[20] Now, strictly speaking, the doctrine applies in the first instance to God *qua* creator, and it is in such terms that Locke usually affirms the doctrine in relation to Him (although he does sometimes employ 'making'

---

19. Richard Ashcraft suggests that 'on this point, Locke never changed his mind' (*RP*, p. 258).
20. The argument that warrants our use of this broad sense of making is presented in the next section.

when referring to God's title, as the passage from I, 53 quoted previously indicates). Thus, some commentators actually identify the maker's right doctrine as a theory of 'creationism.'[21] On the present interpretation, this is at best an unfortunate piece of nomenclature, since, as we shall demonstrate in the next section, Locke also applies the doctrine to men, and men cannot literally create anything. But God, of course, does create and so it seemed worth recalling that the scope of the maker's right doctrine, as we have construed it, embraces the attribution of rights to Him on that basis.

Locke's use of the doctrine of maker's right in II, 6 and I, 53 is such that the doctrine plainly must be ascribed to him in order to license an inference present in the text. Much more direct evidence, however, is available from his *Essays on the Law of Nature*. There, in his sixth essay, 'Are men bound by the law of nature? Yes,' Locke upholds the doctrine of maker's right directly, as a doctrine. In the course of explicating the source of man's obligation to obey the law of nature, Locke argues that 'this obligation seems to derive partly from the divine wisdom of the lawmaker, and partly from the right which the Creator has over his creation.'[22] A little further on, Locke's appeal to what we have called the maker's right doctrine is even more explicitly formulated:

> not all obligation seems to consist in, and ultimately to be limited by, that power which can coerce offenders and punish the wicked, but rather to consist in the authority and dominion which someone has over another, either by natural right and the right of creation, as when all things are justly subject to that by which they have first been made and also are constantly preserved . . . .[23]

On the face of it, it may seem that what God is here credited with on the basis of His creation is a right, not of property, but rather of *sovereignty*; and that, indeed, it is in virtue of His sovereignty that men are obligated to obey the law of nature. But this is a misleading impression, one that derives from the essential ambiguity of the Latin term *dominium*. As Richard Tuck has explained, *dominium* in the natural law tradition

---

21. Ashcraft, *RP*, pp. 258 ff., and Waldron, *RPP*, pp. 198–201.
22. Locke, *ELN*, sixth essay, f. 84, p. 183.
23. Locke, *ELN*, sixth essay, f. 85, pp. 183–85. Locke also recognises here the rights of donation and of contract.

means *both* property and sovereignty.[24] We may thus elect, in a given context, to gloss *dominium* as indicating either property or sovereignty,[25] but what we may not do is to gloss it as indicating property *as opposed to* sovereignty (or vice versa).[26] Therefore, when Locke argues that God's *dominion* is founded on the right of creation,[27] there can be no doubt that he sought to explain the property which God enjoys in all Creation in the terms suggested by the workmanship interpretation.

Given this argument, the role played by the maker's right doctrine in Locke's analysis of natural law is perhaps already apparent. We have seen that, on Locke's analysis, the prescriptive authority of natural law is derived from the fact that man is God's creation. Speaking more precisely, we can now say that man's obligation to obey the law of nature, that is, to obey God's will, obtains correlatively to the right which God enjoys in man, that is, correlatively to His dominion over man. For, as Locke argues,

> we must understand that no one can oblige or bind us to do anything, unless he has right and power over us; and indeed, when he commands what he wishes should be done and what should not be done, he only makes use of his right. Hence that bond derives from the lordship [*dominio*] and command which any superior has over us and our actions. . . .[28]

In other words, God's will is binding on men because of His dominion over them, that is, because men are his property. An explanation of man's

---

24. 'Cumberland had argued rather weakly on the basis of his account of property that the existing distribution of *dominium* (by which he explicitly meant both property and political power, as did most people in the tradition) . . .' R. Tuck, *Natural Rights Theories: Their Origin and Development* (Cambridge: Cambridge University Press, 1979), p. 171; cf. p. 61.

25. Compare the following passages from Tuck: 'already by the fourteenth century it was possible to argue that to have a right was to be the lord or *dominus* of one's relevant world, to possess *dominium*, that is to say, *property*' and 'But it was of course tantamount to the repudiation of the whole history of rights as *dominia*, as active rights expressing their possessor's sovereignty over his world.' *Natural Rights Theories*, pp. 3, 160.

26. We should not confuse this issue, about the concept of *dominium*, with a quite distinct issue raised by Locke in the *First Treatise*. There he argues that property does not confer sovereignty, but by this he clearly means that property *in goods* does not confer sovereignty *over men*. Cf. I, 41.

27. '*sed potius in potestate et dominio illo quem in alium aliquis habet, sive jure naturae et creationis.*' Locke, *ELN*, sixth essay, f. 85, pp. 182–84.

28. Locke, *ELN*, sixth essay, ff. 83–84, pp. 181–83.

natural law obligations, therefore, requires an explanation of God's right or dominion in them and it is to this end, as we know, that Locke employs the doctrine of maker's right. It will thus be observed that Locke's use of this doctrine is central to his analysis of natural law.

Further evidence of Locke's adherence to the maker's right doctrine as the basis of God's dominion is to be found in the *Essay*: 'That God has given a Rule whereby Men should govern themselves, I think there is no body so brutish as to deny. He has a Right to do it, we are his Creatures' (II.xxviii.8). What emerges particularly clearly in the *Essay* is that Locke treats this doctrine as self-evident.[29] Locke here compares the certainty with which its conclusion may be known to that which characterises certain immediately self-evident propositions.

> He also that hath the Idea of an intelligent, but frail and weak Being, made by and dependent on another, who is eternal, omnipotent, perfectly wise and good, will as certainly know that Man is to honour, fear, and obey GOD, as that the Sun shines when he sees it. (IV.xiii.3; cf. I.iv.13; IV.iii.18)

That Locke took the doctrine of maker's right to be as obvious and certain as this is of some significance because it helps us to account for his common practice—manifest, for example, in II, 6—of leaving it as an unformulated premiss of his argument.

Additional assistance on this score is provided by the recognition that use of the maker's right doctrine as the foundation of God's dominion was widespread in Locke's day. This has been well documented by Tully and Ashcraft. In *A Sober Enquiry into the Nature, Measure, and Principle of Moral Virtue*, published in 1673, for example, Robert Ferguson maintains that '"all those duties either to God or man" which are imposed upon us by religion, "we are obliged to by the rule of *creation*."'[30] Similarly, Richard Baxter argues in *A Holy Commonwealth, or Political Aphorisms upon the Principles of Government* (1659) that 'God's kingdom

---

29. This is not meant to obscure the fact that it also enjoys this status in *ELN*. See fourth essay, ff. 58–59, p. 157: 'for who will deny that the clay is subject to the potter's will, and that a piece of pottery can be shattered by the same hand by which it has been formed?'

30. Ashcraft, *RP*, p. 56, quoting *A Sober Enquiry*, pp. 29, 51.

is ... constituted primarily by ... His *right*, resulting immediately from His being our creator, and so our *owner*.'³¹ Indeed, such a deduction of the divine dominion is the one offered, according to Richard Cumberland, by 'most others.'³² Locke, then, would thus have had still further reason to assume that explicit reference in his argument to the maker's right doctrine was unnecessary.

The doctrine of maker's right also lies at the heart of Locke's project, in the *Essay* and elsewhere, of working out a demonstrative science of ethics.³³ Perhaps not surprisingly, the general structure of Locke's analysis here closely parallels that given in the case of natural law.³⁴ The basic idea which informs his project is that of deducing a system of ethical theorems and conclusions from certain self-evident propositions, which owe their axiomatic status to their being commands of God. Men are under an obligation to conform their actions to these axioms (and hence to morality, which follows from them) because of the fact that men are God's workmanship and so his property. The prospect of such a demonstrative science is thus squarely founded on, inter alia, the maker's right doctrine, a point which Locke himself makes in the *Essay*, albeit once again indirectly.

> The Idea of a supreme Being, infinite in Power, Goodness, and Wisdom, whose Workmanship we are, and on whom we depend; and the Idea of our selves, as understanding, rational Beings, being such as are clear in us, would, I suppose, if duly considered, and pursued, afford such Foundations of our Duty and Rules of Action, as might place Morality amongst the Sciences capable of Demonstration: wherein I doubt not, but from self-evident Propositions, by necessary Consequences, as incontestable as

---

31. Tully, *DP*, p. 42, quoting *A Holy Commonwealth*, 3.28. Emphases added.
32. R. Cumberland, *A Treatise on the Laws of Nature*, tr. J. Maxwell (London: R. Phillips, 1727), p. 320. Quoted in Tully, *DP*, p. 42.
33. For a discussion of Locke's project and a fuller accounting of textual references, see G.A.J. Rogers, 'Locke, Law, and the Laws of Nature,' in *John Locke: Symposium Wolfenbüttel 1979*, ed. R. Brandt (Berlin: Walter de Gruyter, 1981), pp. 146–62.
34. Compare the final paragraph of Locke's unpublished essay, 'Of Ethics in General' (quoted in Rogers, 'Laws of Nature,' p. 149) with *ELN*, fourth essay, f. 52, p. 151. The passages are too long to reproduce here. See also Dunn, *Political Thought of John Locke*, pp. 187 ff.

those in Mathematics, the measures of right and wrong might be made out, to anyone that will apply himself with the same Indifferency and Attention to the one, as he does to the other of these Sciences. (IV.iii.18)[35]

The particular details of how this project was meant to be carried out (a task which Locke began, but never pursued very far) are not especially important here. For our purposes, it suffices to note that Locke counts the maker's right doctrine among the foundations of this science.[36] That he does so is a further (although not necessarily distinct) indication of the fact that he took the doctrine to be a self-evident one.[37]

Man as Maker

So far we have been considering the doctrine of maker's right in terms of the broad sense of 'making.' In this sense, making some thing is to be understood in Locke's general causal sense of bringing that thing into being (II.xxvi.2). Now, something can be brought into being either ex nihilo or from pre-existing materials. In Locke's technical vocabulary, 'making ex nihilo' is properly known as 'creation.' Strictly speaking, then, making always begins from pre-existing materials (II.xxvi.2).

Since God brought man into being ex nihilo, it follows that, in the technical sense, He did not make man, but rather created him.[38] We have seen in the previous section that, on Locke's view, God's creation of something entitles Him to a property in it. Man's property, however, cannot be founded on a right of *creation*, because man is incapable of bringing anything into existence ex nihilo.

---

35. A substantially similar suggestion appears in Locke's journal entry of 26 June 1681: '[H]e that has a true idea of God of himself as his creature of the relation he stands in to god and his fellow creatures and of Justice goodness law happynesse &c is capeable of knowing moral things or having a demonstrative certainty in them.' MS. Locke, f. 5, fos. 78–83. Quoted in Tully, *DP*, p. 29.

36. Cf. Dunn, *Political Thought of John Locke*, p. 26. 'Whenever he began to sketch out the contours of an ethic and searched for the fundamental form which it must take, the touchstone which he set up was always the relation between Creator and created.'

37. Cf. Tully, *DP*, p. 42.

38. 'God has created us out of nothing and, if He pleases, will reduce us again to nothing.' Locke, *ELN*, sixth essay, f. 88, p. 187.

> The Dominion of Man ... in the great World of visible things ... however managed by Art and Skill, reaches no farther, than to compound and divide the Materials, that are made to his Hand; but can do nothing towards the making the least Particle of new Matter, or destroying one Atome of what is already in Being. (II.ii.2)

Man, that is, cannot create.

Nevertheless, Locke does claim that it is in virtue of his similarity to God that man is capable of dominion (I, 30, 40). On the workmanship interpretation, man's capacity for property is to be explained in terms of the similarity between man and God as makers in the broad sense. This similarity is itself due to the similarity between making and creating, of which man and God are respectively capable.[39] In each case, on this interpretation, a right arises in the product newly brought into being, namely, a maker's right. Thus, even though he cannot create, man as maker can still bring new things into being and is therefore entitled to a property in them.

Still, there will be an important difference in the logic of the entitlement in the two cases. This difference reflects the fact that making, in the technical sense, always begins from pre-existing materials. For with making, unlike with creation, there is always a prior question concerning the maker's entitlement to the materials from which she begins. In Locke's theory, as we have seen, this question arises in the form of what we have called the consent problem. Since Locke's solution of this problem requires that appropriation be subject to the proviso that enough and as good be left for others, making something is clearly not a sufficient condition of having a property in it.[40] Entitlement to something one has made depends further on the satisfaction of this proviso. In man's case, then, making is only a necessary condition of property, whereas in God's case it is also sufficient.

We have already seen that, insofar as it concerns God and creation, the workmanship interpretation is corroborated decisively by Locke's texts. However, given the strict distinction between making and creat-

---

39. It is because the fundamental appeal of the workmanship interpretation's analogy is to the similarity between making and creating that the force of the analogy, such as it is, is strictly independent of God's existence.

40. Indeed, this follows simply from the fact that this prior question always arises.

ing, this is not sufficient to show that Locke held to what we have called the doctrine of maker's right. It remains to be seen, in other words, whether Locke invokes the doctrine specifically with respect to *man* as maker.

The project of a demonstrative science of morality that Locke announces in the *Essay* was never completed. Nevertheless, there is some manuscript evidence that it was in fact begun.[41] Of particular interest is a manuscript piece entitled 'Morality.' The piece is undated, but Thomas Sargentich has suggested that 'since it is highly hedonistic, it was probably written relatively late in Locke's life.' A late dating helps the argument, but it is not essential. In any case, in 'Morality,' Locke advances the following argument:

> Man made not himself nor any other man. Man made not the world which he found made at his birth. Therefor noe man at his birth can have noe right to any thing in the world more than an other.[42]

This argument constitutes a clear case of the maker's right doctrine being applied specifically to man. A number of points bear notice in this connection. First, of course, the premisses and the conclusion of Locke's argument here are mediated by the assumption that making is a necessary condition of property. It is especially noteworthy that Locke makes this assumption in the context of an exercise in the demonstrative science of morality, in which conclusions are supposed to be deduced 'from self-evident Propositions, by necessary Consequences, as incontestable as those in Mathematics' (IV.iii.18). Second, Locke's first premiss respects the use to which his distinction between man and person is put by the workmanship interpretation, namely, that it is God who makes and so owns man, as opposed to man's person. Third, the qualification 'at his birth' in the conclusion obviates the possibility that 'making' in this argument simply functions sloppily as a synonym for 'creating.' If that were

---

41. Rogers comments that 'the results are hardly exciting, nothing to suggest that Locke could ever have become the Newton of the moral sciences, but the notes suggest that Locke was serious in his intentions.' Rogers, 'Laws of Nature,' p. 150.

42. 'Morality' (MS. Locke, c. 28, ff. 139–40) is published in T. Sargentich, 'Locke and Ethical Theory: Two MS. Pieces,' *The Locke Newsletter* 5 (1974), pp. 28–31. This quotation from Locke appears on p. 29; previous quotation from Sargentich appears on p. 24.

the case, the conclusion would have to be that 'no man *ever* can have any right to anything.' But Locke's conclusion is, rather, the more limited one that no man can have any right to anything *at his birth*, a conclusion which manifestly countenances the possibility that a man might come to have such rights in the course of his life. It follows that the sense of 'making' in question here is the sense on which man is capable of making, that is, the technical sense. We may conclude, then, that Locke does apply the doctrine of maker's right, not only to God but also to man.

The 'Morality' manuscript is straightforward and important evidence for the workmanship interpretation. Still, it would be disappointing if no evidence for this interpretation's account of man's property in particular could be adduced from the text of the *Two Treatises* itself. Fortunately, this is not our situation: for Locke's refutation, in the *First Treatise*, of Filmer's claim that 'Fathers, by begetting them, come by an Absolute Power over their Children' (I, 52) is very obviously informed by the assumption that the doctrine of maker's right applies to man.

In order to see this, it will perhaps be helpful to sketch first the structure of Locke's argument (I, 52–5) and then to fill this sketch out with reference to the text. Locke is concerned to deny Filmer's conclusion that fathers have an absolute power over their children. The power in question here is sovereign power, but Filmer's contention is that fathers are sovereign over their children because they own them. 'There is one thing more, and then I think I have given you all that our A. brings for proof of Adam's Sovereignty, and that is a Supposition of a natural Right of Dominion over his Children, by being their Father' (I, 50). The implication of ownership is introduced by the supposed foundation in a right of *dominion*. Unlike its Latin counterpart *dominium*,[43] the term *dominion* does not invariably imply ownership.[44] But it is plain from the surround-

---

43. Compare Tuck's discussion of a passage in a sixteenth-century text (Fernando Vazquez y Menchaca's *Controversiarum Illustrium*, 1559), in which the claim that parents have *dominium* over their children is clearly taken as implying *ownership* of them. Tuck, *Natural Rights Theories*, p. 51.

44. It would appear that the meaning of the term was already somewhat more mutable in English than it had been in Latin. To judge only by Locke's own usage, it seems that *dominion* could sometimes function simply as a synonym for *property* (e.g., I, 29) and othertimes could function simply as a synonym for *sovereignty* (e.g., II, 54). Often the immediate evidence is not sufficient to determine whether *dominion* means property only,

ing context that we cannot remove that implication in this case. Two things make this plain. First, the power conferred by the dominion is compared to 'that of Absolute Monarchs over their Slaves' (I, 51); and second, the next candidate foundation for this same power that Locke goes on to consider (I, 56–9) is the argument of those 'who alledge the Practice of Mankind, for exposing or selling their Children, as a Proof of their Power over them' (I, 56).

Filmer's argument to the conclusion that fathers own their children may be represented in terms of the following pair of premisses: first, anyone who makes something thereby acquires dominion over it, and second, fathers make their children (I, 52). The major premiss of his argument, then, just is the maker's right doctrine. Hence, a special urgency attaches to Locke's refutation here. As Nozick has well observed, 'Locke must discuss Filmer in detail, not merely to clear the field of some alternative curious view, but to show why that view doesn't follow from elements of his own view, *as one might suppose it did*' (*ASU*, p. 287).

Locke's strategy is to repudiate the second premiss, that fathers make their children. He advances three grounds for doing so. These grounds are nested, in the sense that the subsequent grounds are intended to be sufficient to defeat Filmer even if it is supposed, *arguendo*, that the previous ones do not hold. This strategy is evidently dictated to Locke by the fact that he accepts the only other premiss of Filmer's argument, the maker's right doctrine, and may indeed be taken as evidence of that fact. However, what establishes this point beyond doubt is that, in the course of introducing his final ground for rejecting the second premiss, Locke effectively affirms Filmer's major premiss. Let us consider these grounds in turn.

The first ground on which Locke argues that fathers do not make their children is that man lacks the knowledge and skill required 'to frame and make a living Creature' (I, 53). 'How can he be thought to give Life to another, that knows not wherein his own Life consists? Philosophers are at a loss about it after their most diligent enquiries; And Anatomists, after their whole Lives and Studies spent in Dissections . . . confess their

---

sovereignty only, or both property and sovereignty. In the case at hand, however, the immediate evidence is sufficient to rule out the middle option, as we argue in the text.

Ignorance' (I, 52; cf. 53). Still, even if it is supposed that man had this knowledge, Locke denies that fathers make their children on the second ground that, for the most part, men do not, in sexual intercourse, have the intention of begetting a child:

> But had Men Skill and Power to make their Children, 'tis not so slight a piece of Workmanship, that it can be imagined they could make them without designing it. What Father of a Thousand, when he begets a Child, thinks farther then the satisfying of his present Appetite? (I, 54)[45]

Finally, even if it is supposed that parents do make their children, Locke points out that it does not follow that fathers *alone* make their children, which is what Filmer's conclusion requires. 'For no body can deny but that the Woman hath an equal share, if not the greater' (I, 55). But notice, crucially, how Locke introduces this final objection: 'But grant that the Parents made their Children, gave them Life and Being, and that hence there followed an Absolute Power. This would give the Father but a joynt Dominion with the Mother over them' (I, 55). What Locke argues here is that even if all the objections to the claim that men, that is, human beings, make their children are dropped, Filmer's conclusion still does not follow. For what follows is that the two parents have joint dominion over the children. Now, although this conclusion is sufficient to refute Filmer, *it* only follows from the granted premiss in conjunction with Filmer's major premiss, the maker's right doctrine. Therefore, in affirming *arguendo* the premiss that parents make their children and affirming the conclusion that parents thereby have joint dominion over their children, Locke manifests his affirmation of the maker's right doctrine. Of course, Locke does not, in fact, accept the relevant minor premiss, and so is not committed to the resultant conclusion. But this truth leaves his commitment to the major premiss and hence our interpretative conclusion undisturbed.

It might be objected that this reading of I, 55 misconstrues the scope of that which Locke is granting for the sake of argument. What Locke grants to Filmer for the sake of argument, so the objection might go, is

---

45. Locke actually denies further that the presence of the relevant intention would be sufficient to constitute making, claiming that 'indeed those who desire and design Children, are but the occasions of their being' (I, 54).

not only the minor premiss but the drawing of the conclusion as well. This is to say that *both* 'that the Parents made their Children' and 'that hence there followed an Absolute Power' should be read as falling under the scope of 'But grant . . . .' If this were the case, then Locke's argument on this point could not be counted as evidence of his acceptance of the doctrine of maker's right.

This objection is mistaken. The conclusion 'that hence there followed an Absolute Power' cannot be included under the scope of what is granted for the sake of argument because to do so would violate Locke's nesting arrangement. His argument is structured so that each subsequent objection begins from the assumption (made for the sake of argument) that the conclusion of the previous objection does not hold. Thus, the second objection begins from the assumption that man does have the knowledge required to make children (what the first objection denied). Likewise, the third objection should begin simply from the assumption that parents just do make their children (what the second objection denied). Notice that the third objection need not begin from the more particular assumption that men do (sometimes) have the intention of begetting children (which the second objection begins by denying), for this was already granted in the second part of the second objection:

> And indeed those who desire and design Children, are but the occasions of their being, and when they design and wish to beget them, do little more towards their making, than Ducalion and his Wife in the Fable did towards the making of Mankind, by throwing Pebbles over their Heads. (I, 54)[46]

The only conclusion there remains to deny from the second objection, then, is 'that the Parents made their Children' (I, 55). Consistency with Locke's own procedure therefore requires that we read the beginning of I, 55 as granting no more than this.

One small further problem might occasion concern. The right Locke here says would result from the parents' (counterfactual) making is 'an Absolute Power' (I, 55), whereas—as we shall see—the property which Locke holds that men actually acquire is very far from absolute. Two explanations suggest themselves. One is that this is merely a slip on

---

46. Indeed, these two parts of the second objection might be seen as constituting distinct objections. So doing would still preserve Locke's nesting arrangement.

Locke's part; there is at least one other passage in which Locke, clearly mistakenly, describes man's property as absolute (II, 123). A second explanation is that here Locke carelessly follows the form of Filmer's argument too closely. The formulation is, in any case, surely inconsequential; in the recapitulation which follows immediately, Locke reverts to the terminology of 'Dominion' (I, 55), which has been explicitly marked off from an absolute right (I, 39).

Not only does Locke's discussion in these passages evince his acceptance of the doctrine of maker's right, it also corroborates the workmanship interpretation's connection of this doctrine with his analysis of making in the *Essay*. Recall that it is a part of this interpretation that making is an activity with an intellectual dimension. It is, specifically, one in which a maker designs the product of her making and which is governed by her idea of the product to be made. Locke, it will be observed, contends that fathers do not *make* their children precisely on the grounds that their begetting lacks both of these features: fathers lack the knowledge to design a child (cf. III.vi.3; III.vi.40) and in begetting they lack the intention of producing a child.[47]

Locke's texts do therefore warrant our attributing to him the doctrine of maker's right as an explanation of man's property in particular.[48] Before drawing our final conclusions with respect to the workmanship interpretation, however, we will do well to consider whether any difficulties stand in our way.

Some Objections

In his recent book *The Right to Private Property*, Jeremy Waldron devotes some space to criticising Tully's workmanship interpretation. Waldron, as we have noted, represents the maker's right doctrine as a doctrine of *creator's* rights: 'there are serious difficulties with Tully's interpretation of property rights as creators' rights' (p. 198). This is more than a simple

---

47. Cf. Tully, *DP*, p. 59.
48. Thus, we can now confirm that Locke applies the doctrine both to creating and to making (in the technical sense) and so our recourse to a broad sense of 'making,' comprising them both, was not without justification.

nomenclatural error, for Waldron's criticism actually turns on describing the doctrine in this way. His criticism is that interpreting Locke's labour mixture theme in terms of creator's rights 'yields a conclusion which is far too strong' (p. 198) because, according to Waldron, the rights to which creators are entitled are absolute rights. Hence, if men were to acquire property in virtue of their creation, the property they would thereby acquire would be an absolute one. '"God-like" creation would give us God-like rights over objects, and that (certainly on Tully's own account) is far too strong for the property rights that human appropriators are supposed to have' (p. 199). Consequently, Waldron rejects the workmanship interpretation.

Although the passage which Waldron adduces (I, 53) does not establish this point, it does seem fair to say that creator's rights are absolute ones.[49] Nevertheless, it does not follow from this that the rights to which men are entitled by their labour must, on the workmanship interpretation, be similarly absolute, unless we follow Waldron in conflating the distinction between making and creating. Since, in fact, men cannot create anything, it is difficult to see why they should be entitled to absolute rights in anything on that basis. The rights to which men are entitled in virtue of their *making*, on the other hand, are clearly not absolute. For one thing, the act of making something is not on its own even sufficient for a property in that thing. It is a further distinct necessary condition of enjoying a property in something one has made that one satisfy the enough and as good proviso.[50] As we shall see, this further condition alone introduces crucial limitations in the property which men may enjoy. Thus, we need not be troubled by Waldron's criticism.

The argument of the last section, it will be recalled, involved an appeal to Locke's refutation of Filmer's view that fathers have absolute power over their children. Locke's refutation, so I suggested, is centred on the

---

49. The full sentence says only, 'He that could do this [sc. create], might indeed have some pretence to destroy his own Workmanship' (I, 53). But compare Locke, *ELN*, sixth essay, ff. 88–89, p. 187: 'God has created us out of nothing and, if He pleases, will reduce us again to nothing: we are, therefore, subject to Him in perfect justice and by utmost necessity.'

50. Strictly speaking, this condition should be given as a disjunction. The other disjunct is that one obtain everyone else's consent.

rejection of Filmer's minor premiss, the claim that fathers make their children. On Nozick's analysis, however, this reading of Locke's refutation cannot be right (*ASU*, pp. 287–89). In fact, his analysis threatens the entire workmanship interpretation.

Nozick does not himself endorse any particular reading of Locke's argument, nor does he deny that Locke appears to adopt the strategy we have attributed to him. What he holds, rather, is that this strategy is deeply problematic and so cannot really be what Locke is arguing. The problem, as Nozick sees it, is that Locke's refutation

> seems to depend upon the view that one owns something one makes only if one controls and understands all parts of the process of making it. By this criterion, people who plant seeds on their land and water them would not own the trees that then grow. . . . Yet in many such cases, Locke does want to say that we own what we produce. (*ASU*, p. 288)

In other words, on Nozick's understanding, the criterion by which Locke rejects Filmer's claim that fathers make their children is one which, if consistently applied, would lead to the conclusion that men do not make (and so do not own) many things which Locke does want to say they own (or, at least, could own). This reading presents an obvious problem for the workmanship interpretation. It seems unlikely that Locke would have held both that men's property is to be explained in terms of the doctrine of maker's right and, implicitly, that men do not make many of the things which they are supposed to be capable of owning.

The first thing to be said about this problem is that it brings out well an important respect in which the traditional interpretation of the labour mixture theme is inadequate to Locke's text (I, 52–5). To see this, let us distinguish the process of making something from that of mixing one's labour with it. All making processes can also be identified as mixing processes, but not all mixing processes can also be identified as making processes. This much is clear on any plausible criterion of what counts as a making process. Now, on the traditional view, the logic of property entitlement is founded on a mixing process. Still, as Nozick (who follows the traditional view) has observed, 'ownership rights in what one has made would seem to follow from Locke's theory of property' (*ASU*, p. 287), since any making process is also a mixing process. The difficulty with the traditional view is that it cannot account satisfactorily for the evident restriction of Locke's concern specifically to the refutation of the claim that fathers *make* their children. Locke's aim in I, 52–5 is to disprove Filmer's contention that fathers own their children. But, if the traditional view is correct, a demonstration that fathers are incapable of making their children will not suffice to disprove this contention, since some mixing processes are not making processes. Hence the possibility remains that a father might simply be said to have mixed his labour with his child, without having *made* the child.[51] Only if Locke takes the logic of property entitlement to be founded on a making process is the argument he actually makes against Filmer adequate to his purpose.

This, of course, does not itself resolve the problem for the workmanship interpretation. The key to that lies with Locke's criteria for determining whether someone qualifies as having made something. The criterion which Nozick imputes to Locke is that someone makes something just in case he 'controls and understands all parts of the process of making it' (*ASU*, p. 288). As Nozick would have it, this condition includes, inter alia, complete knowledge of the deliverances of the ideal physics.[52] But the text (I, 52–4) manifestly does not warrant ascribing a condition as strong as this to Locke. On the interpretation of these passages we have offered, Locke's central criterion for determining whether someone has made something is whether he knows what that thing is (I, 52, lines 16f.), in the sense of knowing its real essence. Locke affirms that men have this knowledge in the case of the products of their making (III.vi.40) and denies that they have it in the case of human beings (III.vi.3).[53] Thus, this interpretation of Locke's criterion fits the requirement of his argument without issuing in Nozick's radical conclusion.[54] Furthermore, not

---

51. The point is not that the traditional view leaves Locke without a reply here, but rather that Locke is oblivious to the necessity of making one, a necessity that would arise if he took the logic of property entitlement to be founded on a mixing process, as the traditional view has it.

52. Nozick, *ASU*, p. 288: 'Who knows *all* of what physicists say is relevant to materials having the properties they do and to forces working as they do; and who knows what the physicists don't know?'

53. The best that men can attain in the latter case is knowledge of the nominal essence; only God (i.e., man's maker) can know man's real essence (III.vi.3).

54. This is contrary to Waldron, *RPP*, p. 199.

only does it have support in the text, it also allows us to read Locke's argument there at face value.

The problem Nozick's analysis appeared to pose does not arise, then, because his reading of Locke's criterion for what counts as making is far too strong. Still, there is a real difficulty here, one which does not depend on any misreading of the text.

A Difficulty

The difficulty may be brought out as follows. On the workmanship interpretation, the property a man enjoys in the product of his labour arises in virtue of his having made that product. Property rights so explained, however, are clearly restricted to the kind of things it is possible for a man to make. In other words, it is a consequence of the workmanship interpretation of Locke's theory that property is restricted to the domain of *artificial* things, where artificial things are simply the class of all things which are 'made' in the technical sense.[55] Now, some—indeed, the most important—of the examples of property Locke discusses in chapter 5 are unquestionably artificial things: labour itself; cultivated fields; bread, cloth, and wine. Nevertheless, other examples of his are quite obviously not artificial things: notably, the spontaneous products of nature (acorns, apples, water) and animals. These belong to the class of what we might call, for convenience, *natural* things. So the difficulty is that even though (private) property in natural things cannot be explained on the doctrine of maker's right, Locke plainly includes property in some natural things among the *explananda* of his theory.

It may be helpful to frame this difficulty slightly differently. In order for a thing to count as the sort of thing in which man can have property (i.e., as an artificial thing), it must be plausible to see that thing as having been brought into existence by man.[56] Recall that the essence of an artificial thing is given by the idea or description under which it is brought

---

55. 'When the cause is extrinsical, and the Effect produced by a sensible Separation, or juxta Position of discernible Parts, we call it Making; and such are all artificial things' (II.xxvi.2).

56. Brought into existence, of course, from pre-existing materials.

into existence by its maker. Something counts as artificial, therefore, only if it can plausibly be identified under a description which fixes its membership in some artificial species (cf. III.vi.41).[57] Thus, property in land, say, can be explained on this model because it is plausible to see a cultivated field as something which the labourer has brought into existence. The difficulty is that with some of Locke's examples, such as water and acorns, it seems that no description is available under which they might plausibly be identified as something artificial.

The advantage of putting the difficulty in this way is that it allows us to bring out clearly the bounds of the problem, for it is not as if there is no point at which animals and the spontaneous products of nature can be identified as belonging to some or other artificial species. Whenever they are employed as inputs in any kind of productive process, an appropriate artificial description will eventually become available. So, for instance, by the time apples have become apple pie or applesauce, it will no longer be implausible to see them as something artificial in the relevant sense. In fact, in the case of animals, it is arguable that the process of domestication brings something new into existence and hence that domesticated animals belong to artificial species; it is unarguable that butchered animals do. The real problem, then, is not that property in animals and the spontaneous products of nature cannot be explained on the maker's right doctrine, but rather that Locke simply awards property rights in them prematurely, that is, well before the required identification as something artificial can plausibly be made.

Having thus set the difficulty before us, we need to ascertain exactly for whom it constitutes a difficulty. In particular, we need to determine whether this difficulty manifests a weakness of the workmanship interpretation or, alternatively, whether it manifests a weakness of Locke's theory itself. We shall argue that this is a difficulty present in Locke's own theory.

The first argument for this conclusion is a negative one, that is, one

---

57. Membership in an artificial species is not necessarily inconsistent with (continuing) membership is some natural species. Thus, from the evident fact that a roast duck, e.g., is a member of an artificial species, it follows, no doubt, that the entity in question is an 'ex-duck,' but not that it is no longer a duck at all (i.e., no longer a member of some natural species).

which provides a reason for not seeing the difficulty as a weakness of the workmanship interpretation. The reason is that, unlike the difficulty which plagues the traditional interpretation,[58] the difficulty of explaining how property arises in natural things prior to their entry in productive processes is not very grave and so charity in interpretation does not here require us to fault the interpretation in order to save the theory. Two considerations diminish its gravity. The first is that, as we have noted, the difficulty only obtains for relatively unimportant cases of property. The second and more important consideration is that the difficulty can be neatly bypassed by the following strategy. Instead of explaining property in animals and the spontaneous products of nature directly on the maker's right doctrine (and thereby landing ourselves in the familiar difficulty), we can explain it indirectly on the supposition that property in land (which can be explained without difficulty) encompasses property in animals and so on. The warrant for so doing is Locke's own endorsement: 'But the chief matter of Property being now not the Fruits of the Earth, and the Beasts that subsist on it, but the Earth itself; as that which takes in and carries with it all the rest' (II, 32).

The second argument for charging this difficulty to Locke's account, as it were, is that no interpretation of Locke's theory will be able to handle without difficulty all the cases he presents. With at least one of the examples in the text, Locke has, on any interpretation, awarded property rights prematurely. This is the example of the property in the hare which has not as yet even been caught. 'And even amongst us the Hare that any one is Hunting, is thought his who pursues her during the Chase' (II, 30). The point is that Locke was evidently disposed to extend the application of his theory simply for the sake of completeness, even at the cost of compromising its logic.

The final argument begins from the point that, from the pre-interpretative standpoint, the application of Locke's theory to the cases in question has a certain amount of independent implausibility. Think of the relevant part of Locke's theory simply as being that property is explained

---

58. The difficulty which plagues the traditional interpretation, it will be recalled, is that the conclusion of the argument it constructs does not follow from the premisses it supplies, while the crucial premiss among these arguably begs the question.

by labour, and bracket the questions of how labour is to be understood and why it confers property. If we now ask why it is that a man owns this apple he has picked or that draught of water he has drawn, the reply that in each case the property arises because of his labour will be somewhat implausible. Picking an apple from a tree and drinking from a stream do not strike us as very compelling instances of *labour*.

Now on the traditional interpretation, of course, this pre-interpretative implausibility of Locke's theory is simply dispelled. The logic of the labour mixture model is such that the mixture of one iota of the labour one owns with materials lying in common is sufficient to generate a property in them. Since no one will deny that picking an apple is an instance of labour, the suggestion that it involves the mixture of at least one iota of labour is eminently plausible. Whether it is a compelling instance of labour no longer matters. This is perhaps a merit of the traditional interpretation.[59]

By contrast, the workmanship interpretation reproduces and explains the pre-interpretative implausibility. Thus understood, Locke's theory is implausible when applied to these cases directly because so applying it requires us to treat as artificial things items which are not yet plausibly seen as such. But this does not give us reason to fault the workmanship interpretation, since the implausibility in question clearly originates with the theory itself.

We conclude, then, that the difficulty which arises on the workmanship interpretation of Locke's theory is one which merely reflects a genuine difficulty in Locke's own account, one generated by his overly extended application of the theory.

An Asymmetry

Thus far we have seen that there is ample and impressive evidence for reading Locke as holding to a doctrine of maker's right as the explanation of property. In particular, we have seen that Locke applies the doctrine to the explanation both of God's property and of man's property, and that he does so both in the *Two Treatises* and in other writings, early

---

59. *Perhaps* a merit because the logic it employs to dispel the implausibility is, in fact, fallacious.

and late. Furthermore, we have seen that this same doctrine also underpins the natural law framework in terms of which Locke's discussion in the *Two Treatises* is set. We have argued, on the basis of this evidence, that the labour mixture theme of chapter 5 should be read as a metaphor for the maker's right doctrine.

The chief advantage of the traditional interpretation lies in its literal and thus straightforward reading of the significance of labour mixture. Nevertheless, the traditional interpretation does suffer from a number of disadvantages, at least one of which, so we shall suggest, is decisive. To begin with, it has to distinguish sharply between the explanation of God's property and that of man's property, for there is no denying that Locke explains God's property in terms of a maker's right. What is more, it has to allow that in some places, notably I, 52–5 and 'Morality,' Locke holds to the maker's right doctrine as an explanation of man's property. That is, incredibly, it has to allow that Locke offers two distinct explanations of man's property. Finally, the traditional interpretation cannot assimilate the maker's right passages to the terms of its own account. It is not possible, in other words, to reduce the maker's right explanation of property to the labour mixture explanation (by claiming that the latter explains the former), and thereby to restore a single explanation to Locke's text. This is because there is at least one property that can be explained in terms of a maker's right but that manifestly cannot be explained in terms of labour mixture, and that is the property that a man has in his actions, that is, in labour itself.[60] Hence, the traditional interpretation is forced to burden the text with twin explanations of man's property.

The argument that the labour mixture passages in chapter 5 should be read as a metaphor for the maker's right doctrine does not suppose that this reading makes the best sense of these passages considered in isolation. It maintains, rather, that given the existence of other passages in which Locke holds to the maker's right explanation of man's property, and given the possibility of the metaphorical reading, reading the former passages continuously with the latter ones makes the best overall sense of this part

---

60. Notice that the reason why property in labour cannot be explained on the mixing model is not that we cannot concoct some story on which labour emerges from a mixing process, but rather that, except at the risk of a regress, we are not entitled to suppose that the inputs to any such process include something that one *owns*.

of Locke's theory. No corresponding option is available to us on the traditional interpretation. It is in this asymmetry and in the resultant unity and coherence of Locke's theory and texts that the decisive superiority of the workmanship interpretation lies.

The Preservation of Property

We have now completed our interpretation of Locke's argument for the legitimacy of the institution of private property. It remains only to notice that, in Locke's view, the property regime thus established in the state of nature, while legitimate, is nevertheless incomplete, for the theory of property which Locke propounds in chapter 5 establishes only 'how Labour could at first begin a title of property in the common things of Nature' (II, 51).[61] These natural titles which labour begins are indeterminate and the enjoyment of them is 'very unsafe, very unsecure' (II, 123).

Natural property is quite literally indeterminate because

> the Law of Nature being unwritten, and so no where to be found but in the minds of Men, they who through Passion or Interest shall mis-cite, or misapply it, cannot so easily be convinced of their mistake where there is no established Judge: And so it serves not, as it ought, to determine the Rights, and fence the Properties of those that live under it. (II, 136)

The insecurity of natural property is partly due to this indeterminacy, which fosters 'Controversie about Title,' partly to the fact that men are 'no strict Observers of Equity and Justice' (II, 123), and partly to the 'pravity of mankind,' which is 'such that they had rather injuriously prey upon the fruits of another mans labour . . . than take pains to provide for themselves.'[62] Also, this insecurity is exacerbated by the 'straitning' of some, which is occasioned by the scarcity of land.[63] And so

---

61. Compare II, 30: 'this original Law of Nature for the beginning of Property, in what was before common.'
62. J. Locke, *Epistola de Tolerantia*, 1765, 21, 56–57. Quoted in Laslett, ed. note to II, 124, *Two Treatises of Government*, p. 396.
63. Perhaps it is even brought on by this scarcity; Locke suggests that such disputes and difficulties are absent in the age of abundance (II, 39, 51).

to avoid these Inconveniences which disorder Mens Properties in the state of Nature, Men unite into Societies, that they may have the united strength of the whole Society to secure and defend their Properties, and may have standing Rules to bound it, by which everyone may know what is his. (II, 136; cf. II, 222)

Property and its rights are rendered determinate through the civil codification of the natural property regime:[64] 'in Government the Laws regulate the right of property and the possession of land is determined by positive constitutions' (II, 50; cf. II, 30). It is plainly a condition of success here that men's properties 'become subject to the Government and Dominion of [their] Commonwealth' (II, 120).[65]

Hence, the property which a man owns in civil society can be seen as the *completion* of a property which was inaugurated by natural appropriation and which survives his entrance into that society.[66] '[T]he several Communities settled the Bounds of their distinct Territories, and by Laws within themselves, regulated the Properties of the private Men of their Society, and so, by Compact and Agreement, settled the Property which Labour and Industry Began' (II, 45; cf. II, 38).[67] Thus, in civil

---

64. Any civil organisation of the property which men held in the state of nature, as it must interfere with that property to some extent, is necessarily a consensual process.

65. 'For it would be a direct Contradiction, for any one, to enter into Society with others for the securing and regulating of Property: And yet to suppose his Land, whose Property is to be regulated by the Laws of the Society, should be exempt from the Jurisdiction of that Government' (II, 120). There is nothing in this paragraph that corroborates Tully's contention that 'it follows, *a fortiori*, from his liberty or natural power to dispose and order his person, actions, and possessions being yielded to, and under the direction of, the community, that his possessions also belong to the community' (*DP*, p. 164). Notwithstanding the fact that this liberty is not abjured, but only submitted to the regulation of the community (contrast II, 129 with 130), Tully's argument fails since, by parity of reasoning, it must issue in the absurd conclusion that a man's actions and person also belong to the community.

66. This is contrary to Tully, *DP*, p. 100, and Olivecrona, 'Locke's Theory of Appropriation,' p. 231, who want to drive a wedge between the natural and civil property regimes, whereas the whole thrust of Locke's analysis of property calls for continuity between the two.

67. 'A more plausible reading takes the "settlement" of a system of property to be the provision of those conditions necessary for it to become a permanent and stable basis for economic relations: the drawing up of precise boundaries, the setting up of systems of titles that, in large measure, will eliminate needless disputes and the establishment of

society, governments settle the bounds of, regulate, and protect the properties which men began in the state of nature: that is, they preserve men in their property (II, 124).

---

judicial and executive agencies to resolve any difficulties that remain and to secure entitlements effectively against the threat of violation.' Waldron, 'Locke, Tully, and the Regulation of Property,' p. 104.

II

Limitations of Lockean Property

4

Limitations of the Original Theory

Thus far I have concentrated on interpreting Locke's argument for the legitimacy of private property. I turn now to consider what kind of private property right can be established with this argument. In order to do this I shall have to take account of two different sets of considerations.

To begin with, there is the question of which particular kind(s) of determinate private property right, if any, Locke's argument sanctions. I have to this point been employing 'private property' in the general sense of a right entitling an individual to decide what is to be done with a thing. But, as we have seen in chapter 1, private property in this sense is an indeterminate right. It is, then, as yet an open question whether a more determinate private property regime is legitimated by Locke's argument. It will prove convenient, if somewhat artificial, to distinguish two aspects of this question: first, whether Locke's argument legitimates any specific rights in property, and second, whether Locke's argument imposes any conditions of its own on the legitimacy of the private property rights it establishes.

In addition to these considerations, there is also the question of how far Locke's argument succeeds in establishing that private property is legitimate. We can distinguish two aspects of this question as well: first, how far Locke's argument succeeds on its own terms, and second, how far it succeeds on contemporary terms. I shall clarify in a moment what is meant by success 'on its own terms.' The latter aspect of this question I shall postpone until the next chapter.

Ultimately, my interest lies in the juncture of the two sets of considerations—that is, in ascertaining what particular kind(s) of private property right, if any, can still be successfully established on Lockean grounds. To arrive at that point, I shall proceed as follows. I shall take as my point of departure Locke's own position regarding the determinate kind of private property right sanctioned by his argument. Let me introduce the term *Locke's property* to refer to this right. I shall argue that the specific rights comprised by Locke's property—what we shall call its *nature*—are rather limited, while the special conditions imposed on the legitimacy of Locke's property—what we shall simply call its *conditions*—are not inconsiderable.

Locke's own position on this question, however, is not fully consistent with the logic of the argument on which it is based. It is therefore possible to criticise the conclusions Locke draws from his own argument without thereby impugning the argument itself. So doing allows us to consider how far the argument succeeds on its own terms. Let me introduce a second term, *Lockean property*, to refer—in this chapter—to the determinate kind of private property right that the argument in the *Two Treatises* actually succeeds in establishing. I resort to this extra term as a means of marking the fact that while Lockean property is the right that follows from the logic of Locke's argument, it is not so affirmed by Locke himself. Its introduction should thus serve to avert confusion. I shall argue that the limitations of Lockean property are even greater than those of Locke's property: not only is its nature more limited, but the conditions of its legitimacy are also more extensive.

In the next chapter, I shall consider a contemporary version of the Lockean argument and shall then have occasion to reformulate somewhat the definition of Lockean property. In this chapter, my interest is confined to the argument of the original Lockean theory and the limitations of the private property right that it establishes.

Limits in Locke

The Nature of Locke's Property

In attempting to determine the specific rights in land, say, that one of Locke's landowners enjoys in virtue of his property right, it will be instructive to refer to Honoré's analysis of full individual ownership, component incidents of which are listed in chapter 1. Full individual ownership may be taken as a concrete index against which Locke's property can be assessed. There is no need to assume, in thus making use of Honoré's analysis, that Locke was familiar with all of the incidents deemed standard by Honoré, nor even that those incidents with which Locke was familiar correspond exactly to the standard ones (although they will obviously be closely related, since the history of English property law is one of the central cases on which Honoré's analysis is founded). Honoré's analysis can simply serve as a point of reference in terms of which Locke's remarks can be organised.

One manner of proceeding would be to enquire, for each of the eleven standard incidents, whether its inclusion in Locke's property is required by the argument of the *Two Treatises*. However, this would be tedious and there is no guarantee that a conclusive analysis exists for each or even most of the standard incidents. In practice, the debate has tended to focus on a number of particular incidents, notably the right of free alienation (included in Honoré's right to the capital).

The source of the difficulty is Locke's almost complete silence on the details of this question. His explicit remarks are confined to the stipulations that a property is that which cannot be taken from a man without his consent (II, 138, 140, 193) and that it is a right of use (I, 39, 86–7, 92, 97; II, 31, 34, 36–8, 46, 51), specifically use 'to any advantage of life' (II, 31). Yet, 'Locke is unexplicit about quite what rights people thereby get; nor does he say anything about their duration or their bequeathability.'[1]

Tully suggests that no further rights over the product are conferred by Locke's property beyond this minimum specification (*DP*, pp. 121–24). 'It is a right of use only, not of use, abuse, and alienation' (*DP*, p. 61). However, the crucial issue here is in just what use consists. Without this knowledge, it is not possible to draw the line between use and abuse, or, for that matter, to decide whether alienation counts as a use to the advantage of life.[2]

---

1. Ryan, *Property and Political Theory*, p. 17; cf. p. 45. Locke does explicitly affirm the rights of inheritance and bequest, although not in chapter 5. We ignore this fact for the moment. Ryan is mistaken on this point.

2. Waldron, in 'Locke's Account of Inheritance and Bequest,' p. 44, observes that Locke seems in II, 46 'to be operating with an idea of private property that includes the free right of alienation.'

The way in which the term 'use' should be construed is not at all straightforward. For example, as Honoré has it, the right to use is a distinct incident, separate from the other ten. Honoré suggests that on a wide interpretation of 'use,' this incident overlaps two others—the right to manage and the right to the income (although on a narrow interpretation these are excluded).[3] Whatever one's interpretation on this point—itself no obvious matter, as the three incidents clearly are conceptually distinct—the implication is that the right to use does not entail the eight other incidents (which is confirmed by the practice of liberal societies).

It is not necessary to make the strong claim here that 'use' *cannot* be stretched to cover these incidents. It is sufficient to highlight the space that exists between a use right and a full individual property, space which needs to be bridged by argument. For in principle, there are many different constellations of rights which can be underpinned by the notion of use. One such arrangement is illustrated by Honoré's example elsewhere of a primitive people faced with one of their own who claims full individual ownership of a fishhook he has invented. Their reply is:

> We recognize that you have a right to the fish-hook but not that your right has the unlimited content which you ascribe to it. You ought to explain how to use it and allow each of us to do so in turn. Naturally, as the maker and the inventor you are entitled to a greater share in the use than the rest of us individually, and if you like to call that share 'ownership' we shall not object.[4]

Others are easily imaginable. A maker's right argument such as Locke's does not itself privilege one particular system of use rights over other possible arrangements, although other considerations in his larger argument may rule out some candidates.[5]

In fact, the problem is even broader than this, for we also have to account for the issue of duration, which encompasses the standard inci-

---

3. Honoré, 'Ownership,' p. 168.
4. A. M. Honoré, 'Property, Title, and Redistribution,' in *Making Law Bind* (Oxford: Clarendon Press, 1987), pp. 221–22.
5. 'Once Locke had argued to his own satisfaction that property was not held as a gift from the supposed heirs of Adam, nor with the consent of all mankind, he was unconcerned to argue for any particular sort of property rights, as opposed to any particular attitude to one's possessions.' Ryan, *Property and Political Theory*, p. 45.

dents of transmissibility and of absence of term.[6] Here we can distinguish two questions. One is simply whether the property initially acquired must be one of unlimited duration. It is difficult to see why this should be the case. Patents and copyrights, which also obtain in virtue of a maker's right, are interests which have only a determinate term.

The other question concerns the differential durability of the things in which property is held. In the case of immediate-consumption goods (acorns, apples), the duration of the exercise of the property right is so short that the gap between a use right and a full individual property is obviated. However, in the case of durable goods, and, a fortiori, in the case of land, the battery of rights required to secure use (even minimally defined as personal enjoyment) is much more elaborate: 'the degree of control needed in order to put these things to their proper use is such that I need some guarantee that no one else will make off with my cloak, or climb into my bed as soon as I cease to be in immediate physical occupation.'[7]

It is a mistake to suppose that for the latter goods the uses sanctioned by Locke's argument must be assimilable to those sanctioned for the former ones. The range of possible uses and associated rights is fundamentally different. Why should the respective proprietary interests implied by a maker's right be any less different?

The essential point in all of this is that a use right in property is multiply ambiguous: a wide space exists between a minimal and a maximal construal of it, where a maximal construal corresponds perhaps to full individual ownership. One could therefore accept, without pain of contradiction, that a labourer—even one who satisfied some sufficiency condition—was entitled to rights of use in her product and, further, that it could not be taken from her without her consent, and yet reject the conclusion that she was entitled to full individual ownership.[8]

In order to bridge this gap, that is, to specify the incidents of ownership to which a labourer is entitled, one of two things is required. Either

---

6. Honoré, 'Ownership,' pp. 171–73.
7. Ryan, *Property and Political Theory*, p. 35.
8. 'We must not beg the question of how anxious Locke was to generate such rights in any case. The more limited rights we have outlined would be enough to defeat the claims of royal absolutism.' Ryan, *Property and Political Theory*, p. 36.

we need some supplementary argument to the effect that a particular constellation of incidents is superior to others on grounds of utility, economic efficiency, character development, justice, or whatever, or we need genuine social agreement on the preferred constellation. Locke's argument on its own does not establish the inherence of any particular incident of ownership other than the right to use. Locke's property is thus largely indeterminate.

But, as we have seen, this is just Locke's position in the *Two Treatises*. Natural property titles are indeterminate, as are the rights associated with them (II, 136). It is by compact and agreement that the natural property regime is settled in civil society (II, 38, 45): 'amongst those who are counted the Civiliz'd part of Mankind, who have made and multiplied positive Laws to determine Property' (II, 30). Indeed, it is partly on account of this indeterminacy, and the controversy it engenders, that men decide to enter civil society (II, 136).

Locke's property is limited in its nature, then, because it conveys more extensive rights in property only when supplemented either by some other argument or by social agreement. However, its limitation in this respect should not be taken as an indication of some failure in Locke's argument, for that would be to impute to him a more ambitious aim than is warranted by the text.

Conditions of Locke's Property

To some extent, the distinction between the nature and the conditions of a property right is artificial. Only a fuzzy line can be drawn between the incidents of ownership and the conditions under which ownership is legitimate. Yet as long as we bear this in mind, its use here need not be misleading. In this section, I shall be concerned with the conditions under which Locke's owners enjoy their property. Alan Ryan has written that 'The Christian tradition, recognizing property as only conditionally legitimate in the manner of other social and political institutions . . . had emphasized the owner's duties to the rest of the world rather than his rights.'[9] Although Locke departs from this tradition in his emphasis on rights, he retains the traditional emphasis on the conditional legitimacy

---

9. Ryan, *Property and Political Theory*, pp. 18–19.

of property.[10] Foremost among the conditions placed on the legitimacy of a man's property, of course, are those of spoilage and sufficiency. Without repeating the discussion of these conditions in the foregoing chapters, it will perhaps be instructive to draw out some of the ways in which they impinge on property owners.

To begin with, the logic of the spoilage condition—its name notwithstanding—actually imposes a due-use condition on nonmonetary goods, in addition to the requirement that one not allow one's possessions to spoil.[11] This is more obvious in some formulations than in others: 'and how the spending it upon our uses bounded it' (II, 51).

A right confined to use, however specified, surely does not sanction nonuse.[12] Naturally, use is compatible with reasonable periods of nonuse, but the point is that the spoilage condition affords purchase for some provision for lapse of title. 'Lapse of title is not perhaps of great moral importance, but it may be worth noting that legal rules about limitation of actions and prescription embody the idea that an owner who neglects his property may justly be deprived of it.'[13] The homestead system used to settle the North American West, which required a homesteader to work his property for five continuous years in order to gain title, illustrates a further application of this condition.

The manner in which the sufficiency condition impinges on property owners is complex. It is argued below that Locke himself does not take its implications sufficiently seriously. Nevertheless, even on Locke's own interpretation, the sufficiency condition implies an obligation on the part of landowners to employ those without land of their own.[14]

10. Tully, *DP*, p. 99.
11. In fact, even minimally interpreted, the spoilage condition is inconsistent with an aspect of a leading incident of full liberal property, namely, the right to the capital, for this right includes 'the liberty to consume, waste, or destroy the whole or part of it . . . The liberty to destroy need not be unrestricted. But a general provision requiring things so far as they are not consumed by use to be conserved in the public interest would be inconsistent with the liberal idea of ownership.' Honoré, 'Ownership,' p. 170.
12. 'But here, too, Locke is not concerned to show that a man acquires a negotiable freehold interest in the land; what Locke's argument generates is a service tenure.' Ryan, *Property and Political Theory*, p. 35.
13. Honoré, 'Property, Title, and Redistribution,' p. 218.
14. This obligation may also be discharged by simply handing over the means of subsistence.

Honouring this obligation is a condition of the legitimacy of property in land. The obligation obtains with the advent of land scarcity, and thereafter inheres as a permanent feature of property in land.[15] New owners of land—where the (civil) property regime is specified so as to permit such transactions—inherit this obligation, much as children, when they take up their father's land, also inherit the commonwealth to which he had submitted it (II, 73).

In particular, the obligation to employ landless persons requires a landowner to employ as many people, minus one, as his land could have supported if he had not appropriated it. Until his level of employment has reached this point, Locke's landowner has no right to refuse a landless individual employment.[16]

As everyone's natural right to the means of preservation entitles him to produce the means of comfort and support, this is presumably the level at which payment will be made. The details of such agreements would have to be worked out between the two parties. Interestingly, the results of such negotiations are not determinable by a straightforward application of standard bargaining theory, for since any and every landowner is under an obligation to employ as many landless able-bodied commoners as he can,[17] and since each of these landless able-bodied commoners is himself under an obligation to work, neither party in these negotiations will—at least in theory—have any bargaining power.

Charity

The sufficiency and the spoilage conditions are not, however, the only conditions of the legitimacy of Locke's property. Insofar as charity and

15. Land scarcity exists when there is insufficient land remaining to go around and not just when there is absolutely no land remaining.
16. Strictly, the reference units here should be families, but this does not materially affect the point at hand. For the record, it may be worth noting that this conclusion, while correct, stands the problem as it was understood in Locke's day on its head. '[Locke] subscribed to the orthodox position, seemingly confirmed by experience, that unless work was "found" for the poor, and unless they were forced to labour through hunger or reeducation, unemployment and poverty would be *preferred* over a rising standard of living.' E. J. Hundert, 'The Making of *Homo Faber*: John Locke between Ideology and History,' *Journal of the History of Ideas* 33 (1) (1972), p. 18.
17. Where this ability to employ is given by the number of people minus one which the land could have supported had it not been appropriated.

inheritance constitute titles to the means of preservation (I, 42), they also represent conditions placed on Locke's property.

Unlike violations of these first two conditions, though, violations of the obligations of charity and inheritance do not void a property owner's holdings per se. Such a property owner would be liable, rather, to these claims' being enforced against him. Charity and inheritance may thus be thought of as charges or limits on property holdings which, though legitimately acquired, depend for their continuing legitimacy on these obligations' being discharged.[18]

Locke's discussion of charity (I, 42), as we have said, is often misleadingly read as affirming a right of the poor or needy just as such to be provided with the means of subsistence. In fact, the able-bodied poor—regardless of the extent of their need[19]—do not have any right to charity, for they do have the means to subsist otherwise, namely in the form of their *labour*. What they do have is a right, deriving from the sufficiency condition, to be provided with employment.[20]

The right of charity exists to succour the *disabled* poor and needy, a group comprising the naturally disabled and those who, through poverty or misfortune, suffer from temporary disability.[21] This right derives from the fundamental law of nature, which is the preservation of mankind (II, 6, 16, 135). The earth and the inferior creatures were given to mankind in common by God for the purpose of bringing about this preservation

---

18. 'The priority of natural law renders all rights as means to this end, and therefore Locke's account is a limited rights theory.' Tully, *DP*, p. 131.

19. A person who is so badly off that he cannot labour is obviously temporarily disabled and qualifies for charity on that basis.

20. 'This, rightly considered, shows us what is the true and proper relief of the poor. It consists in finding work for them, and taking care they do not live like drones upon the labour of others.' Locke, *Report to the Board of Trade*, p. 383.

21. Cohen is therefore mistaken to suggest 'that Infirm would fare even worse under Lockean common ownership. Common ownership would allow Able to till as much land as he wished without giving Infirm anything, and, unlike the Steiner constitution, would endow Infirm with nothing to offer Able in return for Able's support.' G. A. Cohen, 'Self-Ownership, World-Ownership and Equality: Part II,' *Social Philosophy and Policy* 3 (2) (1986), p. 88. Winfrey, in restricting charity to the latter group, goes too far in remedying the traditional error: 'this charity is owed only to those few who are otherwise industrious but by some calamity find they have "no means to subsist otherwise."' J. C. Winfrey, 'Charity versus Justice in Locke's Theory of Property,' *Journal of the History of Ideas*, 42 (3) (1981), p. 436.

(I, 86–7, 97; II, 25, 172); indeed, the whole matrix of natural rights is subordinated to this end. In the case of the disabled, however, God's intention must obviously be fulfilled in some other way—whence the obligation of charity.

The obligation of charity applies against the surplusage of a man's goods.[22] In principle, therefore, as long as a man is in possession of surplus goods, he has no right to refuse subsistence to the disabled needy, who 'cannot justly be denied' (I, 42). Moreover, as a natural obligation, charitable assistance is a charge on the holdings of property owners that is enforceable by the civil state (II, 135).[23] Enforcement of these rights of charity preserves the property of the disabled needy. In this measure, Locke's property is limited by its liability to sustain the demands of charity.

Inheritance

Notwithstanding his general silence on the details of the question of how the incidents of ownership are to be specified, Locke—as we have noted—does explicitly affirm the rights of inheritance (I, 87–91, 93, 97–8, 102; II, 72–3, 182–4, 190, 192) and bequest (I, 87; II, 59, 65, 72). Furthermore, he suggests, at I, 87, that the latter right has priority over the former: 'that possession, if he dispos'd not otherwise of it by his positive Grant, descended Naturally to his Children.'[24] But oddly, and even apart from the question of priority, 'as far as bequest is concerned, no explicit justification appears in either treatise.'[25] We concentrate therefore on inheritance.

The rationale underlying a natural right of inheritance parallels the

---

22. Cf. Locke, *ELN*, seventh essay, ff. 95–96, p. 195: 'For we are not obliged to provide with shelter and to refresh with food any and every man, or at any time whatever, but only when a poor man's misfortune calls for our alms and our property supplies means for charity.'

23. Cf. Waldron, 'Locke's Account of Inheritance,' p. 45.

24. Although at II, 65, he seems to reverse the priority: 'a Father may dispose of his own Possessions as he pleases, when his Children are out of danger of perishing for want.' See also the discussion in Waldron, 'Locke's Account of Inheritance,' pp. 44–47.

25. Waldron, 'Locke's Account of Inheritance,' p. 42.

one given for the natural right to charity.[26] Unlike Adam, who entered the world a perfect man and who was thus capable 'from the first Instant of his being to provide for his own Support and Preservation' (II, 56), individuals are normally 'born Infants, weak and helpless, without Knowledge or Understanding' (II, 56). This dependency of children is analogous to a temporary disability since it means that they are unable to provide for themselves. Children are therefore entitled to be maintained by their parents (I, 88–9; II, 56).[27]

This right of maintenance is the foundation of the children's right of inheritance (I, 93, 97). Inheritance allows children to continue to receive the maintenance to which they are entitled from their parents' property even after the parents have passed away. Posthumous fulfillment of the parents' obligation to sustain their children is thereby ensured.

Understanding Locke's account in this way naturally leads one to treat the maintenance and inheritance due the children as a charge on the property holdings of their parents, much as charity is. With respect to the children's right of maintenance, this is undoubtedly the correct approach. Hence, this right acts as a further limitation of Locke's property.[28]

Yet with the right of inheritance proper, Locke actually wants to claim more than this. Wherever he speaks of children inheriting their father's possessions, he speaks of their inheriting those possessions *simpliciter*—that is to say, they inherit all of his possessions. This is confirmed by I, 88, where the children's right is said to be 'in the Possession which comes to be wholly theirs, when death having put an end to their Parents use of it, hath taken them from their Possessions, and this we call Inheritance.'[29]

---

26. An argument for inheritance based on tacit consent inferred from the universality of the practice would, as Locke recognises (I, 88), ground only a civil as opposed to a natural right.

27. This is the basis of the suggestion, made previously, that the relevant distributional unit is the family: 'Men are not Proprietors of what they have merely for themselves, their Children have a Title to part of it, and have their Kind of Right joyn'd with their Parents' (I, 88). See also Waldron, 'Locke's Account of Inheritance,' p. 43; Tully, *DP*, p. 133.

28. 'If a child has a *right* to be sustained out of his father's bounty, then the father's liberty to alienate his property is curtailed by the corresponding duty.' Waldron, 'Locke's Account of Inheritance,' p. 44.

29. Locke's conclusion here is inconsistent with both of his positions (themselves inconsistent) on bequest.

The inheritance right envisioned by Locke is one which conserves family holdings in perpetuity: 'No damage . . . can give a Conqueror Power, to dispossess the Posterity of the Vanquished, and turn them out of their Inheritance, which ought to be the Possession of them and their Descendants to all Generations' (II, 184). Short of the suggestion that 'when their Parents leave the World, and so the care due to their Children ceases, the effects of it are to extend as far as possibly they can' (I, 89), there does not appear to be any particular argument advanced for this position.

Limits to Locke

The Limits of Transmission

The particular kind of private property right that Locke takes his argument to sanction is thus a limited right. Its limitedness is partly due to the multiplicity of conditions that attach to its legitimacy and partly due to the limited argumentative purchase it has on most of the standard incidents in terms of which it might be specified. However, in the remainder of this chapter, I shall argue that the kind of private property right that actually follows from the argument in the *Two Treatises*—what I have called 'Lockean property'[30]—is yet more limited than this. Henceforth, then, the discussion adopts a more critical stance towards Locke's argument.

I begin with the question of the extent to which transmission can be included in the specification of Lockean ownership. *Transmission* is being used here in a nontechnical sense to gather under a single rubric various rights of transfer such as inheritance, bequest, gift, and exchange, which are technically distributed between the standard incidents of transmissibility and of the right to the capital.[31]

This question arises because Locke's property is supposed to be indeterminate with respect to the standard incidents of liberal ownership, apart from the right to use, which definitely inheres in Locke's owners. But to hold that Locke's property is indeterminate is to imply that it can

---

30. Recall that the conditions to be stipulated below as limitations of Lockean property are ones that Locke does not himself affirm in the *Two Treatises*.
31. Honoré, 'Ownership,' pp. 170–73.

indeed include these other incidents, *provided* only that some supplementary argument or social agreement can be produced to establish the legitimacy of further specifying Locke's property in this way. This implication depends, however, on the assumption that every possible incident of ownership is, from the Lockean standpoint, a permissible one. It assumes, in other words, that the exigencies of the argument in the *Two Treatises* do not preclude the inclusion of some incidents.

We shall argue that, on the contrary, the scope afforded for the inclusion of transmission in the determination of Lockean property is strictly limited: there is no scope for bequest or for gifts, and inheritance is limited to the posthumous maintenance of children during the period of their dependency, in accordance with their natural right.

In any potential transmission situation there will be two parties, whom we may call the *present owner* and the *potential owner*. The general permissibility of transmission will be constituted by the possibility of there existing two rights, namely, a right of the present owner to transfer her property and a right of the potential owner to acquire that property. *Permissibility* simply defines the limits within which Lockean property may be further determined by supplementary argument or by social agreement: it screens out the incidents whose inclusion is precluded by the exigencies of the Lockean argument. Hence, transmission will be permissible just in case neither of these two rights is so precluded.

The possibility of there being a right of the present owner to transfer her property turns on the possibility of construing transmission as use. This construal is manifestly possible. Indeed, there is good reason to believe that Locke himself construed it this way.[32] Of course, as we have seen, this is hardly necessary or obvious,[33] but for present purposes it is sufficient that it should be possible.

What about the possibility of there being a right of the potential owner to *acquire* that property? To begin with, it is essential to recognise that

---

32. At II, 46, Locke explicitly characterises exchange and the giving of gifts as use (cf. II, 47–48, 50). His assertion of the right of bequest (I, 87; II, 59, 65, 72) also speaks to this point.

33. 'If I find that I have enclosed more land than I can use the product of, the proper course for me is simply to take down my fences, *not* to purport to give away the surplus to my friends and relatives.' Waldron, 'Locke's Account of Inheritance,' p. 47.

this issue is distinct from that of the possibility of there being a right of the present owner to transfer her property. A's giving a gift to B is as much a case of B's acquiring a property as it is one of A's relinquishing one.

Some may argue that B's right of acquisition is (conceptually or otherwise) essentially tied to A's right of transmission. But even if that argument is correct (which is uncertain), it would only show that A's right presupposed B's right, and not that B's right exists. If A's right is held to entail B's, then A's right is plainly a much stronger right than one which does not license any such entailment. Therefore it stands in need of greater justification than it otherwise would have required. Since it is precisely the ground of this (greater) justification that is here in question, appealing to some such entailment does not suffice as an answer.

A can only exercise her general right of transmission in the particular case of B if B already has a right of acquisition. A's prior right of transmission does not entitle her to give B a gift to which B has no right.[34] A's right of transmission is limited, rather, to entitling her to transfer her property to those who have an independent right to acquire it.

It is true that one can distinguish between acquisition as the appropriation of unheld things—I shall call this *original acquisition*—and acquisition as the reception of previously held things from their former owners—I shall call this *acquisition by transfer*. But this distinction does not obviate the need for B's independent right of acquisition. What the distinction records, in the first instance, is a primitive difference between two classes of things, namely, that the members of the latter class, but not the former, are already owned. Its primary significance lies in the following consequence of this primitive difference: legitimate acquisition of members of the latter class, but not of the former, is subjected to an additional necessary condition, namely, the consent of the previous owner of the thing.

If we are to recognise, as a further consequence of this primitive difference, the 'fact' that a thing's membership in the latter class, but not the

---

34. Consider the situation of public office-holders who are forbidden by law from accepting gifts from a certain class of individuals, whom we may call lobbyists. No one will suppose that a lobbyist's undoubted right to transmit her property is itself sufficient to vest in a public office-holder the right to acquire it.

Limitations of the Original Theory

former, vests everyone, ipso facto, with a presumptive right to acquire that thing,[35] then we require some argument for doing so.[36] Recognition of this further consequence cannot be compelled merely on the ground that the primitive difference recorded by the distinction is a significant one, since its significance can be adequately accounted for simply on the basis of its primary consequence.

In the absence of some such argument, then, the question of the potential owner's right of acquisition collapses into an instance of the general question, What entitles an individual to acquire property? As we have seen, Locke's answer is unambiguous: for able-bodied individuals, the only legitimate title is labour by that individual. But, if labour alone entitles able-bodied individuals to property, then property acquired (originally or by transfer) through other means is necessarily illegitimate.[37]

Thus, the possibility of an able-bodied potential owner's having a right of acquisition by transfer must turn somehow on her labouring. Yet, unlike the case of original acquisition, it will not be possible for the potential owner to labour on the object which she would thereby become entitled to acquire by transfer.[38] In order to determine whether this imposes an insuperable difficulty, it will be necessary to attend to the particular circumstances of the various forms of transmission: exchange, gift, bequest, and inheritance.

Consider first the case of exchange. Exchange is unique among the kinds of transmission specified above in being reciprocal. The present owner of a cheesecake, say, is also the potential owner of some money, and vice versa. There is a mutual rather than a unilateral transfer of prop-

---

35. A *presumptive* right because the right so conveyed is clearly defeasible in special circumstances, such as those of public office-holders in relation to lobbyists.

36. Plainly we also need an argument for recognising the consequence that gives the distinction its primary significance. But this is easy to supply, since the requirement of the previous owner's consent trivially follows from even Locke's most restricted definition of property (i.e., that which cannot be taken from one without one's consent).

37. 'To vest the earner's right in somebody else as a result of his death would amount to the creation of an *unearned* right of property—a right *not* arising from the investment of the labour of the person purporting to hold it. Succession, therefore, would undermine the justification of property entitlements on the basis of labour.' Waldron, 'Locke's Account of Inheritance,' pp. 39–40.

38. Even if it were possible, the consent of the previous owner would still be required for her to acquire the object legitimately.

erty. Hence, it is possible, perhaps even plausible, to construe the labour that earned the money as being in some sense equivalent to the labour that made the cheesecake and as thereby entitling the present owner of the cheesecake to acquire the money, despite the fact that she didn't labour on it. Since it is therefore possible for the potential owner here to have a right of acquisition (and given that it is possible for the present owner to have a right of transfer), exchange must be counted among the permissible incidents of Lockean property, at least where there was labour on both sides.

With gifts and bequests, however, it is difficult to imagine on what the potential owner's right of acquisition might be grounded. There does not seem to be any sense in which labour could so entitle her, for these are cases of unilateral transfer. Nor can recourse be made to the rights of charity or maintenance as alternative grounds, for these rights actually entitle their bearer to much more than a right of acquisition subject to the consent of the previous owner. As we have seen, the title to subsistence which dependent children and the disabled needy possess in virtue of these rights is enforceable against the surplus holdings of property owners, who have no right to refuse it. It would thus be misleading to describe this sort of transfer as a gift or a bequest.

The conclusion that must therefore be drawn is that in a Lockean context there can be no right of a potential owner to acquire a gift or a bequest. Hence, the rights of gift and bequest are not permissible incidents of Lockean ownership.[39] The extent to which transmission can be included in the specification of Lockean property is thereby limited.

Finally, there is the case of inheritance. Like gifts and bequests, inheritance is a unilateral transfer. Hence, the possibility of the potential owner's having a right of acquisition here cannot be grounded in her labouring. Nevertheless, in virtue of their dependency, children do have a right of maintenance, which entitles them to the means of comfort and support and which acts as a charge on their parents' property.

---

39. In this respect, Lockean property resembles the system of property entitlements envisioned by H. R. Varian, 'Distributive Justice, Welfare Economics, and the Theory of Fairness,' *Philosophy and Public Affairs* 4 (3) (1975), pp. 237, 244. Varian, however, abjures all forms of inheritance, while Lockean property makes provision for dependent children.

This dependency (and the consequent right of maintenance) is evidently not removed by the passing away of the children's parents. Indeed, it may well be augmented thereby. In the event of their parents' demise, then, dependent children have a well-grounded right to acquire through inheritance a share of their parents' property sufficient to secure their comfort and support.

Insofar, though, as this right arises in virtue of dependency, the children's right is clearly limited to the period of their dependency: adult descendants have no right of inheritance. Moreover, even dependent children are limited, in the extent of what they can inherit, to what is sufficient for subsistence: there is no ground for the inheritance of surplus property. In the state of nature, that part of the parents' estate which, on their demise, exceeds the maintenance requirements of their children reverts to the common.

Inheritance is a permissible incident of Lockean ownership only where it is limited to the maintenance of deceased parents' children during the period of their dependency. In general, then, the inclusion of transmission in the specification of Lockean property must be limited to this form and to that of exchange.

Access versus Appropriation

We turn now to a fuller consideration of the role of the sufficiency condition in limiting the legitimacy of Lockean property. The sufficiency condition enters Locke's argument to solve the consent problem. This it accomplishes by safeguarding the natural right to the means of preservation. Appropriation which preserves the other commoners' right to the means of preservation does not injure them and therefore affords them no ground for complaint.

Nevertheless, one is inclined to suppose that those commoners who find themselves without land in a context of land scarcity may well have a legitimate grievance, their right to be provided with employment notwithstanding. In order for their complaints to have any purchase in a Lockean context, however, it has to be shown that their right to the means of preservation has not in fact been adequately secured.

On the face of it, the most obvious way of pressing such a claim would be to argue that the landless commoners were being denied the opportunity, which they once rightfully enjoyed, to appropriate some land (and thereby improve their lot) and were in that degree injured. Yet, notoriously, this strategy lands one in a hopeless regress that ends with no one being permitted to appropriate anything.[40] The mechanics of this regress operate on the natural right to an opportunity to appropriate, which is presupposed by the objection. The predicament of the first person prevented by land scarcity from exercising this right vitiates the property of the last person to have made an appropriation, whose predicament in turn vitiates the property of the penultimate appropriator, and so on.

This reply appears conclusive, but it proceeds too quickly.[41] What it overlooks is the possibility that the weakness of the original claim lies not in the insight to which it gives expression but in the manner *of* that expression itself. The operation of the regress critically depends on the original claim's being formulated in terms of a right to an opportunity *to appropriate*, for what the argument exploits is the peculiar and fragile nature of such an opportunity. Yet there is no need to articulate the complaint of the landless commoners in these terms.

As we have argued, the natural right to the means of preservation may be seen as an inclusive right of access to the common materials necessary to produce the means of comfort and support: 'So that here was no Priviledge of his Heir above his other Children, which could exclude them from an equal Right to the use of the inferior Creatures, for the comfortable preservation of their Beings' (I, 87). An opportunity to enjoy access, however, is rather more robust than an opportunity to appropriate, and need not degenerate into a Nozickian regress.

Assume for the moment that the access in question includes access to land. The first (and each subsequent) person denied this access by land scarcity can, in principle, be duly accommodated out of the surplus land holdings of some or other previous appropriator,[42] whereas a right to the opportunity to appropriate cannot be accommodated at all in a context

40. Nozick, *ASU*, p. 176; G. A. Cohen, 'Nozick on Appropriation,' *New Left Review* 150 (1985), pp. 104–5.
41. Nozick recognises this, albeit for a different reason. See Nozick, *ASU*, p. 176.
42. Assuming that the whole population could have been sustained under common ownership.

of land scarcity. Even at the extreme, this ex post accommodation in access does not vitiate the previous appropriator's property in its entirety, but merely its surplus element. So the regress never gets going. Of course, the possibility of an accommodation of this sort is closed to Nozick himself, since he confines his analysis to 'permanent and inheritable property rights' (*ASU*, p. 176). However, this is a consideration extrinsic to the logic of the regress.

Notice, furthermore, that although the other commoners' rights do not require this to be the case, the first appropriator need not deny anyone, just in virtue of being first, the opportunity to enjoy an access to the common materials that is equal to her own.[43] For example, a first appropriator who restricted her appropriation to the minimum share required for subsistence would deny no one that opportunity.[44]

Taking Sufficiency Seriously

Locke's own position in the *Two Treatises* is that the sufficiency condition is perfectly compatible with the existence of a class of landless commoners. Given that the sufficiency condition is meant to safeguard a right of access to the common materials, it may be wondered how such a position is in fact tenable.

It will facilitate the discussion if, following W. N. Hohfeld, we distinguish two senses of 'entitlement' or 'right' at the outset. In one sense, one is entitled to something if one has a *claim-right* to it, that is, if everyone else has a duty to refrain from interfering in one's enjoyment of it. In the other sense, one is entitled to something if one has a *liberty*—or, is at liberty—to enjoy it, that is, if no one else has a claim-right to interfere in one's enjoyment of it.

Now, the crucial move in Locke's interpretation of the requirements of the sufficiency condition is his restriction of the kind of access in question. In Locke's framework, men enjoy common ownership of the earth for a specific purpose: the exercise of their prior right to preserve them-

---

43. It is true, but unimportant, that in one sense everyone else is denied the opportunity that the first appropriator enjoyed, namely, that of being the first to choose.

44. It may be worth repeating that no first appropriator is *required* so to restrict her appropriation.

selves. It follows that the only access to the common materials to which men have a claim-right is that sufficient to allow them to produce the means of subsistence. This is the sense of entitlement in which it would be a violation of natural law for anyone to be denied this minimum access.

Property in land just is not a necessary condition of this naturally lawful minimum access, for this is equally provided by a right of employment. It is therefore true that, in this sense, employed, able-bodied but landless commoners are not being denied any of their natural claim-rights— whence Locke's position that they have no grounds for complaint.

Nevertheless, Locke fails to recognise two salient differences between the position of commoners generally under common ownership and the position of landless commoners under land scarcity that justify the complaints of the latter. The first difference is that unlike landless commoners, commoners generally were formerly *at liberty* to enjoy the fruits of the full potential of their labour. In other words, commoners were formerly at liberty to produce not merely their subsistence but a surplus. Moreover, they had a claim-right to keep whatever surplus they managed to produce, subject to the limits of natural property. The upper bound on their standard of living was therefore, in a manner of speaking, internal: set 'by the Extent of Mens Labour, and the Conveniency of Life' (II, 36) and by the limits inherent in natural property.

This manifestly is *not* the position of landless commoners under land scarcity, for their standard of living is further constrained by an external limit set by the minimum measure of subsistence.[45] A right of employment entitles them (in either sense) to no more than this. Landless commoners are not at liberty even to produce a surplus, since their access to the necessary materials depends on the permission of the landowners. Furthermore, where they are permitted to produce a surplus, not only do landless commoners have no claim-right to keep most, or perhaps even any, of the surplus they produce, but they are not at liberty to keep it either. The benefit of labour's abundance—which Locke so celebrates—is therefore placed at the exclusive disposal of the landowners.

45. It is *further* constrained because the minimum measure of subsistence represents, for able-bodied individuals, a lower standard of living than one bounded only by the 'Extent of Mens Labour' and the spoilage and sufficiency conditions.

The second difference is that under common ownership the access to the common materials enjoyed by commoners generally is the same for each commoner. That is, they all enjoy *equal* access, whereas the access to those materials enjoyed by any and every landless commoner is, *ex hypothesi*, radically unequal to that enjoyed by any and every landowner.[46] Notice that the existence of this second difference *does not depend* on the strong (but uncertain) claim that Locke's commoners had a *claim-right* to equality of access per se. It is sufficient to establish this second difference that, as is certain, they were formerly at liberty to enjoy the equality of access which then obtained.

Clearly, then, the natural property regime fails to preserve the access to the materials necessary to produce the means of comfort and support to which each commoner was originally entitled.[47] Moreover, this failure materially harms—both absolutely and relatively speaking—a significant number of these commoners, namely, all those without land of their own. Thus, it is not true that appropriation which satisfies Locke's sufficiency condition does not injure the other commoners, and it follows that they have ample grounds for complaint.

Locke's sufficiency condition is therefore too weak to discharge the function assigned to it in his larger argument, namely, the resolution of the consent problem. The satisfaction of an adequate sufficiency condition is, however, a necessary condition of the legitimacy of natural appropriation and thus of Lockean property. Hence its requirements need to be taken seriously.

In a Lockean context, a sufficiency condition will be adequate if and only if it conserves for each commoner the access to the materials of the earth to which he was originally entitled.[48] The question, therefore, is whether any form of Lockean property is consistent with this require-

46. Further complaints about the new adversity in the power relations in which some commoners stand to others in the state of nature which is thereby introduced are thus justified. See Cohen, 'Self-Ownership,' pp. 80–87.

47. Cf. Macpherson, *Democratic Theory*, essay 12, pp. 120–22.

48. It should be emphasised here that even this original access is limited by the teleological natural law context in which commoners are entitled to it. Nothing in the foregoing analysis impugns the fact that the common was given to the use of the industrious and rational and not to the fancy or covetousness of the quarrelsome and contentious (II, 34).

ment.[49] One way to prosecute this question would be to specify the features which characterise the access to which Locke's commoners were originally entitled and to evaluate various possible forms of Lockean property on that basis. However, the difficulties of producing an exhaustive specification here, even assuming that one exists, are considerable.

Still, a prima facie case can be made that at least one form of Lockean property would satisfy an adequate sufficiency condition. In the absence of an exhaustive specification, this case must obviously remain provisional. But neverless a partial answer to the question is thereby provided, one which leaves open the possibility of other legitimate forms of Lockean property.

In a Lockean state of nature, the sufficiency condition would be satisfied by a regime of Lockean property[50] in land in which each able-bodied commoner had a claim-right to a share of land equal to that of every other able-bodied commoner.[51] This is *not* to say, of course, that vesting such a claim-right in every able-bodied commoner is a *necessary* condition of satisfying the Lockean sufficiency condition, but only that it is a sufficient condition of doing so. Naturally, the realisation of this prior inclusive right in actual Lockean ownership of a particular plot of land would depend on labour on the part of each able-bodied commoner.[52]

Under such a form of Lockean property, each commoner would evidently have sufficient access to the materials necessary to produce the

---

49. Cohen suggests that the answer to this question must be negative and further that 'not only capitalism but every economic system will fail to satisfy a defensible strong Lockean proviso, and that one must therefore abandon the Lockean way of testing the legitimacy of economic systems.' Cohen, 'Nozick on Appropriation,' p. 101.

50. That is, of use rights subject to the limitations previously stipulated (excluding that of the [now otiose] obligation to employ landless commoners) and to those imposed by the sufficiency condition elaborated upon below.

51. We abstract here from the complication of how best to integrate a familial structure (nuclear or otherwise) into the specification of the distributional unit. Disabled commoners continue to be sustained by a right of charity and dependent children by a right of maintenance. Compare Steiner's suggestion 'that the spirit of Locke's exact similarity proviso is captured in the requirement *that each individual has a right to an equal share of the basic non-human means of production.*' H. Steiner, 'The Natural Right to the Means of Production,' *Philosophical Quarterly* 27 (1977), p. 49.

52. This, coupled with the fact that the kind of ownership acquired is Lockean and not full individual property, importantly distinguishes the case at hand from Cohen's 'Steiner constitution.' See Cohen, 'Self-Ownership,' pp. 87–96.

Limitations of the Original Theory 117

means of subsistence. Significantly, each commoner would be at liberty to enjoy the fruits of the full potential of her labour: the benefit of labour's abundance would be at everyone's disposal. Equality of access would also be guaranteed by definition, and thus adversity would be absent along this dimension of the power relations among commoners. In short, it would appear that no one would have any relevant grounds for complaint.

What is important to recognise here is that the legitimacy of this form of Lockean property does not turn on any actual or hypothetical initial equal division of land. That would just reintroduce the mechanics of the consent problem transposed as an organisation problem. It rests rather on the inclusive claim-right which entitles each commoner to an equal share of land. This right limits the de jure property which any commoner has in her de facto holdings to a share which is consistent with every commoner's having the same share. We might say that it limits property in land to the greatest universalisable share.

Thus, in principle, the appropriation of land by individual commoners can proceed piecemeal as described by Locke, except that the Lockean property that appropriators thereby acquire is subject to the further condition that the size of the original holding is open to modification should it subsequently prove not to be universalisable.[53] Commoners who happen to find themselves without land in a context of land scarcity therefore have an enforceable claim to be accommodated out of the definitionally surplus[54] land-holdings of other commoners by just such a modification.[55] This function could manifestly be discharged only by a civil state.

---

53. Thus Steiner's contention in 'Natural Right,' p. 47, that 'Locke's exact similarity proviso requires appropriators to know . . . the number of all (including future) individuals' is mistaken. It is obviously in the interest of appropriators to confine themselves to what they expect will be a universalisable share, but their expectations need not be infallible.

54. A surplus holding must now be defined as one which exceeds the greatest universalisable share, rather than as one which exceeds that required to produce the means of subsistence. The level of comfort and support that can be produced on the greatest universalisable share will be a function of technical knowledge, economic organisation, size of the share, and fertility of land. In the final analysis, the definition of subsistence is similarly a function of these factors.

55. Plainly, landless commoners need not exercise this right if they prefer to labour on someone else's land. A case can probably be made that, within a capitalistic mode of economic organisation, such commoners could alternatively act as rentiers. The market

The Generation Problem

Lockean property is an impermanent right in two senses, first because, subject to a limited right of maintenance, the goods in which it holds revert to the common on the demise of the owner. And second, with reference to land, because the size of the holding is always open to modification, even within the owner's lifetime. The occasion for modifying the size of the universal share is the appearance of landless able-bodied commoners. Land scarcity would constitute just such an occasion.[56] All those who, for one reason or another, had not yet made their own appropriation would then be entitled to be accommodated in this way.

However, the newly defined universal share is no more permanent than the old. This is because, under the reasonable assumption of net population growth over time, the attainment of maturity by each successive generation of commoners will constitute the occasion for further modifications in the size of the universal share. I shall call this the *generation problem*.[57] The difficulty posed by the generation problem is, of course, that the efficient use by any commoner of her share of land presupposes some tolerable degree of stability in the content of that share. This stability is imperilled by the prospect (let alone the fact) of constant modifications in the size of the universal share.

Nevertheless, the important point here for a Lockean theory of property is that, whatever this problem's solution, it cannot take the form of a trade-off. Universalisability is one of the conditions of the legitimacy of this form of Lockean property in land. Hence, the exigencies of accommodating the claims of each new generation have priority over the requirements of the present and ongoing use of such Lockean properties.

---

return on a share of land would be diminished however by the limitations inherent in Lockean property, particularly its non-transmissibility (in the technical sense). See Honoré, 'Ownership,' pp. 171–73.

56. The present analysis abstracts from the complications introduced by distinguishing between local and global land scarcity and hence from those of international relations.

57. A slightly different version of this problem is articulated and discussed by Steiner, 'Natural Right,' pp. 45 ff., and in H. Steiner, 'Liberty and Equality,' *Political Studies* 29 (4) (1981), pp. 558 ff.

None of this itself serves to resolve the generation problem, but only to indicate a constraint that impinges on possible solutions. Proposed solutions may not compromise equality of access to land among contemporary able-bodied commoners. There is, however, no necessary answer to the question of which particular arrangements should be adopted in order to minimise disruptions in land use.[58] Here, too, Lockean property is indeterminate.

---

58. Short of the requirement that *some* arrangement be adopted. The implications of Steiner's discussion—that (1) a part of each new generation will be discouraged (in effect, blackmailed) from exercising their right to an equal share of land by the cost (which they partially bear) of the resulting instability and that (2) the cost of the instability attending the accommodation of the remaining part is morally unavoidable—highlight rather than dispense with this requirement. Steiner, 'Liberty and Equality,' p. 566.

5

A Latter-Day Lockean

Since my aim is to ascertain the particular kind of private property right that can still be successfully established on Lockean grounds, I shall have to relax the constraint, under which I was operating in the previous chapter, of considering only how far the Lockean argument succeeds 'on its own terms.' Relaxing this constraint requires me to bracket the contribution of those premisses of the Lockean argument that are no longer generally tenable and so to consider how far the argument succeeds without their support.

The premisses to be bracketed, of course, are those which rest on theistic assumptions. On the face of it, it might seem that modernising the Lockean argument in this way would simply have the effect of voiding it, since one would thereby be required to bracket its entire natural law framework. But, in fact, this is mistaken on two counts. In the first place, it is a mistake, as I have argued in chapter 1, to suppose that it is the entire natural law framework—as opposed to a subset of natural law premisses—that defines what is characteristic of the Lockean argument. Perhaps more important, it is a further mistake to suppose that any natural law premiss that *Locke* rests, ultimately, on theistic assumptions is, ipso facto, no longer generally tenable. For, as we shall see, it is possible to model in purely secular terms the function discharged in the Lockean argument by that subset of natural law premisses which is characteristic of the argument. Far from voiding it, then, modernising the Lockean argument allows us to consider precisely how far it succeeds on contemporary terms.

In this chapter, I shall examine one contemporary version of the Lockean argument, namely, that advanced by Robert Nozick in *Anarchy, State, and Utopia*. Nozick's version is developed in connection with

A Latter-Day Lockean 121

his entitlement theory of distributive justice, of which it forms a part (pp. 150–82).[1] Except perhaps incidentally, I shall not be concerned here with the issue of the nature of theories of distributive justice. Instead, I shall focus on the justification of private property rights provided by Nozick's entitlement theory.[2] Specifically, I shall enquire whether the particular kind of private property right that Nozick succeeds in establishing is any less limited than Lockean property.

I shall argue that the limits of modernised Lockean property, by which I mean the kind of property right legitimated by a modernised Lockean argument, are substantially similar to those of Lockean property. Nothing in Nozick's entitlement theory has the effect of obviating the limits in the nature of Lockean property, and, while some of the conditions of Lockean property are clearly obviated, the limits of that property which obtain in virtue of the sufficiency condition remain in full force.

Nozick on Property

Locke's account of property has two characteristic elements. One is the apparatus of the consent problem: its generation by the context of common ownership and its solution by the stipulation of the sufficiency condition. The other is the doctrine of maker's right: a labourer is entitled to the product of her labour in virtue of having made it. The integrated argument holds that if the sufficiency condition is satisfied, labourers enjoy a natural property in the material product of their labours (or, what is the same thing, that a natural property is so enjoyed *subject* to the satisfaction of the sufficiency condition).

Although it may not be immediately obvious, since the primary aim of the relevant text is to advance a particular conception of the nature of distributive justice, the basic structure of Nozick's argument about property rights is strikingly similar to Locke's. Consider first the apparatus of the consent problem.

---

1. This and subsequent internal page cites in this chapter to Nozick are to *ASU*.
2. In so doing, I ignore Nozick's own suggestion that he nowhere advances a specific theory of this kind himself (e.g., *ASU*, p. 153). See also Cohen, 'Nozick on Appropriation,' p. 94 and note.

Of course, the consent problem cannot arise in Nozick's theory in the same way it does in Locke's. Although he makes use of the language of natural rights discourse and of state of nature theory, Nozick does not share the background assumptions that inform Locke's seventeenth-century use of this same language. Thus, in particular, Nozick does not employ the natural law postulate of common ownership of the earth from which Locke's analysis begins. Rather, he takes it for granted that, in their original state, natural resources are the property of no one. The principle of justice in acquisition specifies the process 'by which unheld things may come to be held' (p. 150).

Still, in Nozick's state of nature, everyone is initially at equal liberty to use the available unowned natural resources.[3] Within the context of a libertarian theory, this is sufficient to generate a consent problem with respect to the formation of individual property rights. The acquisition by any individual of rights in property changes the moral universe in which everyone else acts. It imposes on everyone obligations that restrict her liberty and that might therefore be thought to require her consent.[4] Hence, it looks as if consent will be necessary to legitimate a natural property regime even without common ownership.

Nozick's argument focuses on the quality, rather than the mere fact, of such alterations in the moral universe: 'This change in the situation of others (by removing their liberty to act on a previously unowned object) need not worsen their situation' (p. 175). In other words, it is only *adverse* restrictions of one's liberty that are rights-violating.[5] Thus the 'crucial point is whether appropriation of an unowned object worsens the situation of others' (p. 175). Where the situation of others is not wors-

---

3. O'Neill contends that Nozick's adoption of what we may call the no-ownership premiss 'does more than eliminate a redundant theological framework.' O. O'Neill, 'Nozick's Entitlements,' in *Reading Nozick: Essays on Anarchy, State, and Utopia*, ed. J. Paul (Oxford: Basil Blackwell, 1982), p. 316. Her contention in 'Nozick's Entitlements,' however, turns on the peculiar use of this framework which she attributes to Locke. See pp. 316–20.

4. See A. Gibbard, 'Natural Property Rights,' *Noûs* 10 (1976), pp. 77–86; Steiner, 'Liberty and Equality,' pp. 566–69.

5. In this respect, Nozick's position must be distinguished from hard libertarianism, which holds 'that it is impossible to deprive someone of a right unless he himself gives up or loses that right through a voluntary act.' Gibbard, 'Natural Property Rights,' p. 78.

ened, there will be no violation of the right to liberty and therefore no need for consent. Hence, within the entitlement theory, following Locke, a sufficiency condition is imposed on rights in property to ensure that the situation of others is not worsened.[6]

Now the content of Nozick's sufficiency condition is clearly determined by what is to count as 'worsening the situation of others.' On the basis of the regress argument we encountered in the previous chapter, Nozick denies that depriving someone of the opportunity to make an appropriation relevantly worsens her situation.[7] Moreover, Nozick maintains that 'someone whose appropriation otherwise would violate the proviso still may appropriate provided he compensates the others so that their situation is not thereby worsened' (p. 178). To worsen the situation of others through appropriation, then, is to worsen *on balance* the situation of those no longer at liberty to use that which has been appropriated.[8]

In order to operate in an argument for property rights, a sufficiency condition such as this must be defined relative to some point of reference. 'The difficulty in working such an argument to show that the proviso is satisfied is in fixing the appropriate base line for comparison. Lockean appropriation makes people no worse off than they would be *how*?' (p. 177). It seems clear[9] that, in terms of the entitlement theory, the relevant point of reference for the sufficiency condition is the state of nature prior to the formation of property rights (p. 181). Nozick's sufficiency condition will be satisfied as long as no one is made worse off on balance than she would have been had the no-ownership situation persisted.

Against this background, Nozick asserts that a private property regime will satisfy the sufficiency condition. 'Here enter the various familiar social considerations favoring private property' (p. 177), whereupon fol-

6. 'Locke's proviso that there be "enough and as good left in common for others" (sect. 27) is meant to ensure that the situation of others is not worsened.' Nozick, *ASU*, p. 175.

7. Nozick, *ASU*, pp. 176–78, as emended by Cohen, 'Nozick on Appropriation,' pp. 104–5. Nozick also excludes the worsening of another's position effected by one's successfully (and, presumably, fairly) competing with her. See *ASU*, p. 178.

8. Cf. Nozick, *ASU*, p. 178n.

9. The uncertainty expressed at Nozick, *ASU*, p. 177, refers to a distinct concern. Cf. Cohen, 'Nozick on Appropriation,' pp. 94–95, 95n.

low 'some familiar empirical theses about the utility of private property, the usual claims about risks, incentives, and so forth which represent capitalism as an especially productive form of economic organization.'[10]

Consider now the other element of a Lockean theory of property: the argument for the particular property rights which may arise given that the sufficiency condition is satisfied. Nozick reads Locke's labour mixture argument of II, 27 in the traditional fashion and disparagingly scrutinises the argument thus interpreted. Yet, oddly, he makes no attempt to rehabilitate it, nor does he advance any alternative account of the ground of the actual titles to property on which the entitlement theory is founded. Nozick restricts himself to the remark that 'whether or not Locke's particular theory of appropriation can be spelled out so as to handle various difficulties, I assume that any adequate theory of justice in acquisition will contain a proviso similar to the weaker of the ones we have attributed to Locke' (p. 178).

Officially, then, the entitlement process remains unspecified. However, despite this lacuna in the official version of his theory, it is worth noting that Nozick appears elsewhere to take the doctrine of maker's right for granted. Indeed, he explicitly asserts what may be taken as a definition of this doctrine: 'Whoever makes something, having bought or contracted for all other held resources used in the process (transferring some of his holdings for these cooperating factors), is entitled to it' (p. 160).[11] This enters into the entitlement theory completely unargued and issues, for example, in Nozick's well-known claim that 'things come into the world already attached to people having entitlements over them' (p. 160).[12]

Thus, at least unofficially, Nozick's argument incorporates both of the characteristic elements of a Lockean theory of property. Furthermore, we should observe here that, at least as far as the question of its tenability in *secular* terms is concerned, there is no reason—as we saw in chapter 3—to exclude the maker's right doctrine from the official argument.

10. Cohen, 'Nozick on Appropriation,' p. 99.
11. Substantially similar assertions are made in *ASU* at pp. 185–87, 225.
12. Cohen in 'Nozick on Appropriation,' p. 92, disputes this claim on the ground that 'people create nothing *ex nihilo*, and all external private property either is, or was made of, something which was once no one's private property.'

(Of course, Nozick may have other objections to its inclusion, but that is, for present purposes, beside the point).

The conclusion that one is entitled to the products of one's making depends on three premisses:

1. If one makes something ex nihilo, then one is entitled to it.
2. Making something from pre-existing materials is sufficiently like making something ex nihilo (so that if one makes something, then one is entitled to it, *provided* no one has a legitimate objection to one's use of the relevant materials).
3. No one has a legitimate objection to one's use of the relevant materials.

Obviously, the plausibility of premisses (1) and (2) will vary inversely with the strength of the entitlements claimed on their basis.[13] In fact, as in Locke's own case, the entitlements claimed under (2) are sure to be weaker than those claimed under (1). But, in any event, what is difficult to deny is that, at some level of entitlement, premisses (1) and (2) retain a certain plausibility, even in our day.[14] What is more, their plausibility is strictly independent of any theistic assumption: even if one substitutes 'creating' for 'making ex nihilo,' and assumes that only God can create,[15] these premisses imply no commitment to theism because (1) is given as a conditional. That is why we said that even Locke's use of the maker's right doctrine to explain man's property is consistent with a secular position.

---

13. We ignore the third premiss here, since it is related to the operation of the sufficiency condition.

14. For a recent discussion of the pervasive influence of (what we have called) the maker's right doctrine in political philosophy, both modern and contemporary, see Ian Shapiro, 'Resources, Capacities, and Ownership: The Workmanship Ideal and Distributive Justice,' *Political Theory* 19 (1) (1991), pp. 47–72. Unfortunately, Shapiro (mis)understands the doctrine as requiring theistic assumptions and thus understands its contemporary influence in terms of successive attempts to secularise the doctrine. Cf. also I. M. Kirzner, 'Entrepreneurship, Entitlement, and Economic Justice,' in *Reading Nozick: Essays on Anarchy, State, and Utopia*, ed. J. Paul (Oxford: Basil Blackwell, 1982), pp. 395 ff.

15. One assumes that 'if x exists, then x can create' holds where 'x' stands for God, and otherwise not.

To return to the official version, Nozick's integrated argument for individual property rights holds that '[a] process normally giving rise to a permanent bequeathable property right in a previously unowned thing will not do so if the position of others no longer at liberty to use the thing is thereby worsened' (p. 178). Notice that, quite unlike Locke, Nozick is fairly explicit about the kind of property right that he takes to have been established: whereas Locke's natural property titles are largely indeterminate, Nozick's property titles are supposed to be permanent and bequeathable. Thus, strictly speaking, they comprise the technical incidents of transmissibility and absence of term—which in estate law are conjoined in the notion of unlimited duration.[16] Moreover, Nozick clearly indicates that these titles further include unlimited rights of transfer:[17]

> Like others, Williams looks only to questions of allocation. He does not consider whether they come already tied to people who have entitlements over them (surely the case for service activities, which are people's *actions*), people who *therefore* may decide for themselves to whom they will give the thing and on what grounds. (pp. 234–35; second emphasis added)[18]

We need not consider how closely the titles Nozick envisions here resemble full liberal ownership, since our main interest concerns the kind of property right that the entitlement theory actually succeeds in establishing.

The Indeterminacy Objection

It may be thought somewhat peculiar that Nozick, an entitlement theorist, does not officially specify the basis of the entitlement process. Of greater significance than its peculiarity, though, is the question of whether this omission affects the strength of Nozick's argument. G. A. Cohen, for one,

---

16. Honoré, 'Ownership,' pp. 171–73.
17. It is unclear whether, within the entitlement theory, the question of rights of transfer belongs to the specification of the principle of justice in acquisition or to that of the principle of justice in transfer. That it arguably belongs to both indicates (what is equally true of the comparable ancient distinction between the problem of acquisition and that of use) that these are not distinct principles of justice in holdings and hence that Nozick's inductive definition is less than perfectly tidy. *ASU*, p.151.
18. Rights of this kind are assumed throughout the discussion of *ASU*, pp. 157 ff.

suggests that everything turns on Nozick's interpretation of the sufficiency condition and therefore that this particular omission is relatively inconsequential.[19]

However, one key feature of the entitlement theory is its historical character: 'whether a distribution is just depends upon how it came about' (p. 153). On this basis, Nozick sharply distinguishes it from what he calls 'end-state principles,' on which the justice of a distribution is determined by its structure. Thus, a central Nozickian claim is that 'an injustice can be worked by moving from one distribution to another structurally identical one, for the second ... may not fit the actual history' (p. 153). Hence, the nature of the entitlement theory clearly requires that individuals be entitled to *particular* holdings (p. 157n).

But, as Onora O'Neill has pointed out, 'no argument yet given explains how one rather than another individual acquires a particular holding.'[20] The sufficiency condition per se, however interpreted, is inadequate to this crucial task. From the fact that a regime of individually held property satisfies the sufficiency condition follows absolutely nothing about *which* individual is entitled to *what* holding within that regime.[21]

Nor may it be replied that if, beginning from a situation of no-ownership, each brute acquisition that satisfied the sufficiency condition entitled the responsible individual to that acquisition, particular entitlements would thereby arise in accordance with the sufficiency condition alone. For supplementing the operation of the sufficiency condition here is a suppressed principle of entitlement by first taking.[22] The doctrine of first taking has, of course, a venerable natural law pedigree, having been employed by Grotius and Pufendorf, among others.[23] Nevertheless, it too requires some argument.[24]

---

19. Cohen, 'Nozick on Appropriation,' pp. 92–93.
20. O'Neill, 'Nozick's Entitlements,' p. 314.
21. That it is a *regime* of property which is justified by the sufficiency condition is even implicit in Nozick's own question, 'Is the situation of persons who are unable to appropriate ... worsened by a *system* of allowing appropriation and permanent property?' (p. 177, emphasis added).
22. Cf. Cohen, 'Nozick on Appropriation,' p. 92: 'Why should B be required to accept what amounts to a doctrine of "first come, first served"?'
23. See Tully, *DP*, pp. 80–82 and 86–87.
24. We shall not enquire here into the merits of this doctrine. For an exposition of

Without a specified principle of entitlement, then, Nozick's theory degenerates into either an unhistorical theory of justice in holdings or a failed, because arbitrary, historical theory. Nozick appears to avoid this dilemma only through his illegitimate (because unacknowledged) reliance on the doctrine of maker's right, which allows him to claim, for example, that 'the situation is *not* one of something's getting made, and there being an open question of who is to get it' (p. 160).

The consequences of Nozick's omission run deeper still. Recall that Nozick takes the kind of property right established by the entitlement theory to be something like a full individual right in the liberal sense. On what grounds are people entitled to rights of this particular kind? In virtue of his omission, it is not open to Nozick to tie the nature of the property in question, namely, the particular complex of incidents in terms of which it is constituted, to the reasons for which entitlement of some form is held to obtain.

Two courses of argument remain open. First, it might be maintained that the rights comprised by full individual ownership were entailed by the concept of private property itself. Thus, once a system of private property had been justified, no further questions about specific rights of ownership would be in order. Assuming that such was the case might constitute a less satisfactory variant of this argument; and, in places, Nozick's rhetorical questioning does suggest that he takes a number of these rights to be self-evident.[25]

But, as we have seen in chapter 1, Nozick also provides a definition of a property right,[26] one on which the concept of private property is, in the absence of a given constrained set of options, simply indeterminate

---

some criticism, within the natural law tradition, of first taking as an entitlement principle, see Tully, *DP*, pp. 86–87.

25. For example, 'If the people were entitled to dispose of the resources to which they were entitled (under D_1), didn't this include their being entitled to give it to, or exchange it with, Wilt Chamberlain?' (p. 161).

26. 'The central core of the notion of a property right in X, relative to which other parts of the notion are to be explained, is the right to determine what shall be done with X; the right to choose which of the constrained set of options concerning X shall be realized or attempted' (p. 171; cf. p. 281).

with respect to the specific rights it conveys.[27] Furthermore, he holds that 'the constraints are set by other principles or laws operating in the society; in our theory, by the Lockean rights people possess (in the minimal state)' (p. 171).[28] This means that the first course of argument is actually closed by the structure of Nozick's own theory, for insofar as the source of the constraints is external, set 'by other principles,' they do not follow from the concept of private property itself.[29]

To make matters worse, Nozick cannot avail himself of any constraints from within the entitlement theory as a means of generating determinate rights of ownership, for the Lockean rights which are the source of these constraints include the rights of protection against theft and fraud, and of enforcement of contracts (p. ix)—in short, rights of property. Nozick therefore lacks a noncircular basis on which to specify a determinate concept of private property.

A second course would be to argue that the rights of full individual ownership are grounded directly in the logic of Nozick's sufficiency condition. This is to say that Nozickian owners are entitled to full liberal rights in their property because regimes of *this* kind are the most productive and thus maximally satisfy the sufficiency condition. But, as we shall see, the sufficiency condition, even on Nozick's interpretation, does not privilege mere brute productivity, but only productivity that realises a distribution of (economic) goods that is Pareto-superior with respect to some comparison-regime. Since various regimes of, for example, less than full individual ownership will severally represent Pareto-optimal distributions of these goods, the sufficiency condition cannot serve to legitimate a regime of full liberal ownership as against other, less extensive regimes of individual ownership. Hence this second course of argument fails as well.

27. This indeterminacy obtains in virtue of the general definition of property and so is not unique to *private* property.
28. Nozick comments here that 'we lack an adequate, fruitful, analytical apparatus for classifying the *types* of constraints on the set of options among which choices are to be made, and the *types* of ways decision powers can be held, divided, and amalgamated' (p. 171).
29. This conclusion should not surprise us, given our argument in chapter 1, nor, therefore, does it depend upon the peculiarities of Nozick's own theory.

Thus, not only is the entitlement theory incapable of accounting for the possession by individuals of particular property holdings, but it is equally incapable of accounting for the inherence of particular *rights* in property. The omission of a specified entitlement process from Nozick's official theory is, therefore, of considerable consequence. Nozick can, of course, remedy these deficiencies by falling back on the unofficial version of his theory, that is, by adopting the Lockean maker's right doctrine. We have seen both that this remedy is available to him and that there is interpretative warrant for it in his text. However, this remedy would obviously not remove any of the limitations in the nature of Lockean property. On this score, then, a modernised Lockean can do no better than the emended original,[30] though she can do rather worse.

Compensation and Comparison

As with Locke's argument, the entitlement theory holds that an individual's property rights are conditional on the situation of others not being thereby relevantly worsened. Specifically, the legitimacy of a right in property requires that the situation of others no longer at liberty to use the thing to be owned not be worse, on balance, than it would have been had the no-ownership situation persisted. Nozick is confident that liberal property regimes cannot but satisfy this sufficiency condition because 'the baseline for comparison is so low as compared to the productiveness of a society with private appropriation' (p. 181).

Nozick's sufficiency condition has two salient characteristics. One is the compensation mechanism in virtue of which 'worsening' is specified as 'net worsening,' and the other is the terms in which having one's situation relevantly worsened is actually defined. For the most part, we shall be concerned with the latter characteristic, although we shall begin with a brief consideration of the former.

By incorporating provisions for the payment of compensation into the structure of the entitlement theory, Nozick legitimises appropriative acts

---

30. This is not to suggest that adoption of the maker's right doctrine is the *only* remedy available to Nozick. But it *is* the only one that preserves his Lockean credentials.

that restrict the liberty of others in some ways, but leave them (in the final analysis) on at least as high an indifference curve as they would have been on in the no-ownership situation.[31] Appropriators may infringe on the liberty of others just because the benefits of a regime of individually held property compensate those others for this loss of liberty, thereby leaving them indifferent between the no-ownership and individual ownership situations.

A number of problems arise here in relation to the issue of compensation. Nozick distinguishes between 'full' and 'market' compensation. Market compensation for a boundary crossing, such as an infringement of liberty, is defined as 'the price that would have been arrived at had a prior negotiation for permission taken place' (p. 65). It is due whenever the crossing in question is a productive one.[32] Since for Nozick the boundary crossings involved in appropriation are extremely productive, market compensation must be due nonappropriators. How is this compensation to be calculated? The essential difficulty is that the market, on which Nozick seems to be relying here, generates outcomes (prices, output, distributive shares) only relative to a given set of initial endowments.[33] Because it is changes in precisely these endowments for which compensation is being paid, there is no noncircular way in which to calculate this compensation in market-derived terms.[34]

Moreover, as Eric Mack has argued, Nozick's use of the compensation mechanism implicitly involves a dramatic shift in the conception of rights underlying the entitlement theory: the deontological basis of rights degenerates into a consequentialist one. 'The shift to this outcome orientation is a product of making the wrong of boundary crossing rest upon

---

31. 'Something compensates X for Y's act if receiving it leaves X on at least as high an indifference curve as he would have been on, without it, had not Y so acted.' Nozick, *ASU*, p. 57.

32. E. Mack, 'Nozick on Unproductivity: The Unintended Consequences,' in *Reading Nozick: Essays on Anarchy, State, and Utopia*, ed. J. Paul (Oxford: Basil Blackwell, 1982), p. 186.

33. A. Sen, 'The Moral Standing of the Market,' *Social Philosophy and Policy*, 2 (2), 1985, pp. 9–14; Steiner, 'Natural Right,' pp. 4–6.

34. Indeed, insofar as full compensation also makes use of market-derived measures (e.g., prices), this point does not turn on the appropriate compensation's being market compensation.

the inadequacies of schemes of posterior compensation for boundary crossing.'[35]

It should thus be clear that Nozick's compensation mechanism is hardly unproblematic. Nevertheless, rather than develop these criticisms, we turn to a consideration of the second characteristic of Nozick's sufficiency condition. Obviously the tenability of defining the notion of 'worsening' in Nozick's terms will bear centrally on the importance of these criticisms.

The criteria in accordance with which Nozick judges someone to be better or worse off are economic. An individual's welfare is reducible to the state of her material well-being, which (in principle) is expressible in terms of the attainable bundles of goods and services among which she is indifferent, given certain assumptions.[36] This much is manifested by the fact that, for Nozick, compensation—which can remedy one's having been made worse off and completely restore a previous state of well-being—is always payable in monetary terms.[37] It follows that to make someone worse off is, in effect, to diminish her net worth.[38]

As a corollary of his conception of individual welfare, Nozick evaluates the net contribution of a regime of full liberal ownership to individual welfare in terms of what we shall call the *productive bounty criterion*. The productive bounty of a property regime is the increase in economic productivity that can be realised by moving to that regime from another, less productive one.

---

35. Mack, 'Nozick on Unproductivity,' p. 186.
36. See Nozick, *ASU*, pp. 57–58.
37. See *ASU*, p. 339, note 7, where Nozick countenances each person's net assets being held in a central computer bank as a sufficient condition of obviating problems of collecting compensation.
38. On Nozick's view, a person is made worse off if the highest indifference curve which she can now reach is lower than the one on which she had been prior to the act in question. An individual's ability to reach any particular indifference curve is determined by her budget line. Thus, relative to a given set of preferences and prices, changes in an individual's highest attainable indifference curve can only be occasioned by changes in the magnitude of the budget line. Of course, significant changes in an individual's net worth may alter the shape and position of her indifference curves, making any such comparisons impossible. This difficulty does not appear to be of concern to Nozick: 'Shamelessly, I ignore general problems about the counterfactual "as well off (on as high an indifference curve) as X would have been if Y's action hadn't occurred"' (p. 57).

The foundations of this criterion, which Nozick fails to elucidate, may be conjectured as follows. Productivity is represented in economic theory by a production-possibility frontier, analogous to the way in which an individual's net worth is represented by a budget line. Furthermore, the role of the production-possibility frontier in social welfare analysis is analogous to that of the budget line in individual welfare analysis. A society's production is therefore one measure of its aggregate net worth.

However, since Nozick's argument is not a utilitarian one (p. 177), each individual's situation must be evaluated separately. It follows that the productive bounty (an outward shift in the production-possibility frontier) of a regime of individually held property must be realisable by a Pareto-superior move. Not only must aggregate net worth increase, but no one individual's net worth may decline. Nozick does not articulate this crucial requirement and appears to *assume* that, for the regimes in question, it is in fact satisfied.[39]

On Nozick's interpretation, then, appropriation by individuals satisfies the sufficiency condition because of its vast productive bounty. What is absolutely pivotal to Nozick's argument, of course, is the selection of the comparison regime. Nozick's basis of comparison, as we have seen, is the no-ownership situation. The productive bounty of the institution of individual ownership equals the difference between the productivity of such a regime and that of one without any form of ownership. Hence, strictly speaking, in order to make use of this criterion one would have to determine the productivity of a no-ownership regime.[40] But Nozick is confident that the productive bounty of individual ownership will be large, regardless of the details of one's calculation.

Cohen criticises Nozick on the grounds that it is arbitrary to restrict the basis of comparison to the no-ownership situation.[41] Nozick *is* guilty of arbitrariness because the legitimacy conferred by the logic of his pro-

---

39. Cf. Cohen, 'Nozick on Appropriation,' p. 100: '[Nozick] would say, of those proletarians who do manage to sell their labour power, that they will get at least as much and probably more in exchange for it than they could have hoped to get by applying it in a rude state of nature; and, of those proletarians whose labour is not worth buying, that, although they will therefore, in Nozick's non-welfare state, die (in the absence of charity), they would have died in the state of nature anyway.'

40. Nozick's uncertainty in *ASU* at p. 177 and note relates to the value of *this* figure.

41. Cohen, 'Nozick on Appropriation,' pp. 95–101.

ductive bounty criterion is not unique to regimes of full individual ownership. For, even accepting Nozick's basis of comparison and terms of analysis, all the argument establishes is that a given regime of property rights is legitimate if and only if moving to that regime from one of no-ownership generates a Pareto-superior productive bounty. There will clearly be many forms of ownership, the legitimacy of which can be established by this criterion, including regimes of communist, market socialist, and less than full individual ownership.

Moreover, it is important to recognise that the productive bounty criterion is incapable of picking out any one of these regimes as being more legitimate than the others.[42] To see this, let us generalise the formulation of the productive bounty criterion thus: for any two regimes of rights in property, A and B, regime B is legitimate with respect to A if and only if moving from A to B generates a Pareto-superior productive bounty. On this more general criterion, a given property regime can be identified as the *most* legitimate regime only if a move to it from every other kind of property regime would generate a Pareto-superior productive bounty. It should be obvious that a regime of full individual ownership will not satisfy this requirement. Consider the various property regimes that can be legitimated with respect to the no-ownership regime. We may suppose that each of these regimes will constitute a Pareto-optimum, since it is very plausible that, in each of them, there will be some individuals who are better off under that particular property regime than they would be under any other.[43] Even if a regime of full individual ownership is the most productive, then, the requirement that a legitimating productive bounty be Pareto-superior will not be satisfied with respect to any of these other property regimes.

42. It will thus be observed that Nozick's sufficiency condition is indeed inadequate to the task, within the entitlement theory, of specifying the particular rights in property that individuals enjoy. This would require discriminating among various regimes of individual ownership, including less than full ones. One such regime is proposed by Varian, 'Distributive Justice,' pp. 237 ff.

43. Cf. Cohen, 'Nozick on Appropriation,' p. 101: 'For there will always be some who would have been better off under an alternative dispensation which it would be arbitrary to exclude from consideration.' Cf. also Sen, 'Moral Standing of the Market,' pp. 9–10.

Beyond Productive Bounty

These criticisms are sufficient to vitiate Nozick's claim to have established a robust legitimacy for full individual rights in property. The entitlement theory, however, is open to a further and more fundamental objection, one which impugns its legitimacy even with respect to a situation of no-ownership. This objection applies in virtue of the Lockean structure of the entitlement theory and descends from our earlier criticism of Locke. Developing the objection here will allow us to demonstrate that modernising the Lockean argument does nothing to remove the limitation on Lockean property imposed by the sufficiency condition.

The foundational move in Nozick's interpretation of the sufficiency condition is the restriction of the evaluation of someone's being better or worse off to purely economic criteria and hence, by extension, of the evaluation of property regimes to the productive bounty criterion. One means of objecting to this restriction, perhaps the most satisfactory one, would be to develop a full-blown critique of the moral reductionism implicit in Nozick's understanding of individual well-being. Nevertheless, it will suffice to object to Nozick's restriction *as* an interpretation of the sufficiency condition. This we will succeed in doing if we can elucidate one important respect in which individuals are worse off under liberal property regimes, without necessarily being compensated therefor, than they would have been in a no-ownership situation.

Ironically, perhaps, one thing individuals stand to lose with the formation of the kind of property regime Nozick advocates is a precious liberty: that of access to natural resources, that is, to means of production. While a propertyless individual in a fully appropriated world may indeed be *permitted conditionally* to use various means of production, she is not *at liberty* to do so, as she would have been in a situation of no-ownership (or, say, in Locke's state of nature).

Nozick attempts to pre-empt this objection by (mis)formulating it in terms which degenerate into a reductio (p. 176). But, as we have already seen, the opportunity to enjoy access to natural resources, as distinct from the opportunity to appropriate them, is immune to Nozick's regress argument. The natural liberty of access to means of production is therefore not a spurious liberty. We can distinguish two aspects of this liberty, neither of which is secured under a regime of full individual property and both of which underline its vital importance. Nozick follows Locke in failing to appreciate either sufficiently.

First, under no-ownership, everyone's liberty of access to the means of production is equal.[44] The significance of this equality arises in virtue of the close connection between the possession of property (a precondition of which is, ultimately, access to means of production) and power: 'Ownership is properly understood as a certain sort of power over things. . . . But ownership can also bring with it various sorts and degrees of power over people.'[45] Equality in the liberty of access to means of production mitigates the inequalities of power over people which can obtain because of an unequal incidence of full individual ownership in things.[46] 'In assessing the gains and losses people sustain following transformations such as the one we are examining, entitlement theorists tend to neglect the value people may place on the kind of power relations in which they stand to others.'[47]

Second, and more important, if we accept the unofficial version of Nozick's theory, the liberty of access to means of production enables everyone to enjoy the fruits of the full potential of her labour.[48] That is

---

44. 'When no external resources have as yet been acted upon by anyone, it is reasonable to think that no one has more right to them than anyone else does.' Cohen, 'Self-Ownership,' p. 94.

45. M. Walzer, *Spheres of Justice: A Defense of Pluralism and Equality* (Oxford: Basil Blackwell, 1983), p. 291. For an illuminating illustration of this connection, see Walzer's discussion at pp. 295–303 of the case of Pullman, Illinois.

46. Cf. T. Scanlon, 'Nozick on Rights, Liberty, and Property,' *Reading Nozick: Essays on Anarchy, State, and Utopia*, ed. J. Paul (Oxford: Basil Blackwell, 1982), p. 118: 'Whether assigning one person the right unilaterally to deny others access to a certain good (say, university education) gives him a morally significant or questionable degree of control over them depends on the role that this good plays in the lives that people lead and aspire to in that society. This question is not settled by asking whether people could have done without the good in the state of nature or by asking how much it is valued by the particular individuals who are involved in a given case.'

47. Cohen, 'Nozick on Appropriation,' p. 96.

48. Since it is Nozick's interpretation of the sufficiency condition that is at issue, nothing turns here on attributing this particular version of the theory to him. Any version which includes a specified entitlement process will do. For the classic discussion of the history of the claim that everyone has a (claim-) *right* to enjoy the fruits of the full

to say, it enables anyone to earn a claim-right,[49] on the basis of the maker's right doctrine, to whatever she has produced. Thus, in particular, everyone is at liberty to produce a surplus and, should anyone do so, she would enjoy a claim-right to that surplus.[50] The production of surplus is made possible by the abundance of labour. Under a regime of no-ownership, this abundance of labour is at the disposal of every able-bodied individual, whereas under a Nozickian regime of full individual ownership, it is at the exclusive disposal of full liberal property owners.[51]

In fact, propertyless individuals are, in some respects, worse off under a Nozickian property regime than they are under even Locke's regime. Given full appropriation, such individuals at least have a claim-right to subsistence employment under Locke's regime, whereas under Nozick's they have no such right. What is more, if no property owner consents to employ them, then they lack even the liberty to produce their subsistence (or to consume it, for that matter)[52]—that is, they have a duty not to do so. Since Nozickian property owners are under no obligation to employ them, the propertyless in his regime, unlike those in Locke's, have lost the *control* they once enjoyed over their access—at the subsistence level—to the means of production. In this respect, then, they are worse off under Nozick's regime than they are under either Locke's or the no-ownership regime.

---

potential of her labour, see A. Menger, *The Right to the Whole Produce of Labour*, tr. M. E. Tanner (London: Macmillan, 1899).

49. The particular kind of claim-right so earned is given by the nature of Lockean property.

50. Notice that under no-ownership, in sharp contrast to the case of full individual ownership, the rights which A enjoys in the surplus that she has produced are the same as the rights which B has in the surplus that she has produced, and so on.

51. Specifically, the owners of the means of production, who specify the conditions on which others are permitted to use them.

52. Compare the memorable passage from Malthus' *Essay on the Principle of Population* (1803) quoted by Menger, *Right to the Whole Produce of Labour*, p. 4: 'A man who is born into a world already possessed, if he cannot get subsistence from his parents on whom he has a just demand, and if society do not want his labour, has no claim of *right* to the smallest portion of food, and, in fact, has no business where he is. At Nature's mighty feast there is no vacant cover for him. She tells him to be gone, and will quickly execute her own orders.'

Notice that along this dimension the propertyless individuals' being worse off is not rectified if, as a matter of fact, they are employed at the subsistence level—as Nozick perforce assumes they will be[53]—since their employment is still contingent on the inclination of property owners, and so beyond their own control. It follows, contrary to Nozick, that a decline in one's net worth is not a necessary condition of one's being worse off.

However, even if the propertyless were to have a claim-right to subsistence employment under Nozick's regime, they would *still* be worse off, with respect to their control over their access to means of production, than they are under the no-ownership regime. This is because under no-ownership everyone's control over her own access to means of production extends to the level of surplus production[54] rather than being curtailed at the subsistence level. By contrast, under Nozick's regime (assuming a fully appropriated world), only the owners of means of production retain this control. The propertyless have a duty not to produce a surplus without the consent of some owner of means of production. No owner of means of production is under an obligation to license a propertyless individual's production of surplus, and should one do so, the propertyless individual has neither a claim-right nor a liberty to enjoy such surplus as she is licensed to produce.

It will thus be readily observed that Nozick's interpretation of the sufficiency condition can be criticised on the same grounds on which we criticised Locke's interpretation of it.[55] Indeed, if anything, these grounds are even more securely established with a *modernised* Lockean argument than they were originally: the modernised argument eliminates the dif-

---

53. Nozick must assume that the able-bodied propertyless will, in fact, be employed at least at the subsistence level because otherwise their net worth would be lower than what it was under the no-ownership regime. In that case the Pareto-superiority requirement on the productive bounty generated by the move to full individual ownership would be violated.

54. This control is conveyed by the liberty, which everyone enjoys, of producing a surplus and the attendant claim-right that inheres in anyone who actually does produce a surplus.

55. Nozick's interpretation can be criticised more heavily on these grounds, since Locke's interpretation at least conserves everyone's liberty of access to the means of production at the subsistence level.

ferentiation, present in the *Two Treatises*, in the commoners' initial entitlement to their access to the means of production. Recall that Locke's commoners have a claim-right to their access to the means of production at the subsistence level, but that their access at the surplus level is 'only' protected by a liberty-right. This differential entitlement does not, of course, license the conclusion that commoners may be deprived, without their consent, of their access to the means of production at the surplus level. Consent is required because depriving a commoner of this access takes something from her to which she was originally entitled by the terms of God's gift and materially harms her in so doing. But although the conclusion rests on a mistake, the mistake may nevertheless seem tempting. The modernised Lockean argument eliminates the scope for this temptation by according a uniform protection to everyone's initial access to the means of production in the state of nature and a greater prominence to the claim that adverse restrictions of one's liberty require one's consent. The limitation that the sufficiency condition imposes on modernised Lockean property, then, is especially clear: the institution of Lockean property is legitimate only if it conserves everyone's liberty of access to the means of production.

Still, not all of the limitations on the legitimacy of Lockean property obtain in virtue of the sufficiency condition. As we have seen in the previous chapter, the legitimacy of Lockean property is also limited by the necessity of satisfying the spoilage condition, the disabled needy's right of charity, and dependent children's right of maintenance (inheritance). In Locke's theory, these limits are ultimately grounded in a premiss of his argument's natural law framework for which there is, and can be, no functional equivalent in a modernised Lockean argument: namely, the premiss that God intends that the earth should serve the preservation of mankind. Since no modernised Lockean theory of property will retain this premiss, modernising the Lockean argument clearly has the effect of removing those limitations on the legitimacy of Lockean property to which that premiss gives rise.

6

Conclusion

I shall conclude by reviewing the main conclusions for which I have argued in the course of this book, as well as the main lines of argument on which I have sought to rest these conclusions. I shall begin this review with a summary account of Locke's argument for the legitimacy of private property, confining myself to a positive statement of my own interpretation. I shall then pass to a recapitulation of the principal arguments I have adduced in defence of this interpretation. Here I shall concentrate on the defence of the more novel or controversial aspects of the interpretation I have presented. Finally, I shall end by cataloguing the limits that inhere in Lockean property and by retracing the argument that establishes these limits as consequences of the logic of the Lockean argument itself.

The Interpretation of the Argument

At one level of description, the aim of Locke's argument is to demonstrate that men can legitimately acquire individual property rights in things in the state of nature. This aim is to be achieved within the theoretical framework given by the natural law tradition. The original condition of the state of nature in this framework is one of positive communism, in which everything is owned by everyone in common. This natural right to property in common, which everyone enjoys, is equivalent to the natural right to the means of preservation. The natural right to the means of preservation ultimately derives from the fundamental law of nature, which enjoins the preservation of mankind. Since the law of nature represents the will of God, it is binding on all men.

In order to achieve his aim, then, Locke has to show that positive communism constitutes no impediment to the legitimate acquisition of individual property rights in the state of nature. Grotius had previously attempted to solve this problem by positing a worldwide compact in accordance with which individual property rights were acquired through universal consent. However, since Grotius' solution had been effectively discredited by Filmer, Locke explicitly sets out to show that this problem can be solved without recourse to universal consent. This is the consent problem.

Although it interrupts the order of Locke's own presentation, we shall proceed immediately to his solution of the consent problem. The presumption that positive communism is an impediment to individual appropriation rests on the supposition that individual appropriation violates everyone's right to property in common. If this supposition is mistaken, however, then the presumption underlying the consent problem will prove to be specious. Locke's strategy, accordingly, is to argue that under certain conditions individual appropriation does not violate anyone's right to property in common and hence its legitimacy requires the consent of no one.

The right to property in common just is the right to the means of preservation. Specifically, it is the claim-right not to be excluded from the use of the common materials needed to produce one's subsistence. If sufficient materials exist for someone to produce his subsistence and if he is not excluded from the use of them to that end, then that person's right to the means of preservation has not been violated. We can put this more generally by saying that no one's right to the means of preservation will be violated as long as sufficient materials are effectively available for everyone to produce his subsistence. This condition, in turn, will be satisfied if (S) *either* there is sufficient unappropriated land remaining for everyone to produce his subsistence *or* every plot of appropriated land is sufficiently productive to sustain as many people as it was capable of sustaining prior to being appropriated, and this many landless individuals (minus one) are permitted access to it to produce (or earn) their subsistence. In other words, no one's right to the means of preservation will be violated as long as (S) obtains. Locke solves the consent problem by stipulating that individual appropriation is subject to the proviso that (S) obtains. We have called this proviso the sufficiency condition.

Locke has thus explained why individual appropriators may legitimately forgo the consent of the other commoners, but he has not yet explained why the appropriation of particular things is legitimate. The interpretatively neutral account of Locke's explanation is that the appropriation of particular things is legitimated by one's labouring on them, subject to certain conditions. This account leaves it open, of course, whence the legitimating power of labour derives. Following Tully, I have suggested that Locke's explanation should be read as holding that the appropriation of particular things is legitimated by one's having *made* them, subject to certain conditions. On this interpretation, the legitimating power of labour derives from what I have called the maker's right doctrine.

The maker's right doctrine can be elaborated in terms of the following premisses.

1. If one creates something, that is, makes it ex nihilo, then one owns it.
2. Making and making ex nihilo are similar processes.

Premiss (1) is supposed to be a self-evident principle. Locke employs (1) to explain God's dominion, that is, property and sovereignty, in mankind and in all of Creation. God's dominion is the basis of mankind's obligation to obey His will, that is, to obey the law of nature; it is also the foundation both of morality and of the prospect of a demonstrative science of morality.

Premiss (2) is to be affirmed because making and making ex nihilo are both species of 'cause,' that is, they both bring new things into being. Furthermore, both processes are governed by the idea of that thing which the maker thereby brings into being, which idea constitutes the thing's essence. Making and making ex nihilo are similar, then, because they are both processes by which a maker effects the material realisation of some idea of his. Of course, since making *ex aliquis* always begins from pre-existing materials, a question arises here that does not arise with making ex nihilo, namely whether the maker is entitled to use the materials from which he begins. But in Locke's theory this question is easily settled, for as long as the sufficiency condition is satisfied, anyone may legitimately use materials lying in common in such a way as to generate a property in them.

From these premises, the legitimating power of labour is held to follow by analogy. What Locke argues is that the appropriation of particular things is legitimated by one's having made them because making *ex aliquis* is sufficiently similar to making ex nihilo that it likewise confers property in what is made on the maker, provided that his use of the relevant materials is itself legitimate.

The individual property rights men may acquire in accordance with Locke's integrated argument are subject to two provisos. The first requires that one appropriate only as much as one can use before it spoils, and is imposed by the law of nature. It obtains, more precisely, in virtue of God's intention that the earth should serve the preservation of mankind and so not be wasted. The second proviso is the sufficiency condition, imposed by the exigencies of avoiding recourse to universal consent in a context of positive communism.

Locke's state of nature is divided into two periods. In the age of abundance, the sufficiency condition is, ipso facto, satisfied, since the first disjunct of (S) obtains: there is sufficient unappropriated land remaining for everyone to produce his subsistence. However, the introduction of money—a legitimate, because consensual, development—issues in the age of scarcity, in which this first disjunct no longer obtains. Nevertheless, Locke argues that even in the age of scarcity the sufficiency condition is still satisfied, now because the second disjunct of (S) obtains: every plot of appropriated land is sufficiently productive to sustain as many people as it was capable of sustaining prior to being appropriated and at least this many landless individuals (minus one) are permitted access to it to produce (or earn) their subsistence.

This final part of Locke's argument turns on an appeal to labour's abundance, that is, to the fact that the productivity of appropriated land is vastly superior to that of common land, ninety-nine times so, on Locke's estimate. Labour's abundance, conjoined with respect for landless individuals' right to subsistence employment, guarantees that the second disjunct of (S) obtains.

As I have summarised it, Locke's argument may seem entirely oriented toward the able-bodied, that is, those for whom access to the materials needed to produce subsistence quantities of meat, drink, and whatnot is sufficient to secure their preservation. But that is clearly not the case: the fundamental law of nature enjoins the preservation of everyone (with the exception of criminals), including those for whom the right to the means of preservation is of no use. Hence, the disabled needy are vested with a natural right of charity, which entitles them to subsistence drawn from the surplus property of others, and children are vested with a natural right of maintenance (inheritance), which entitles them to subsistence drawn from the property (estate) of their parents.

The Argument for the Interpretation

The structure of Locke's argument for the legitimacy of private property is clearly analysable into two distinct substructures. On my interpretation, these substructures have been identified as the apparatus of the consent problem and the doctrine of maker's right. From the standpoint of the argument itself, these substructures are interdependent. Each plays an essential role in the argument. Without the contribution of the former, the legitimacy of using the materials from which making begins—and hence of the acquisition of individual property rights—cannot be guaranteed without recourse to the (impracticable) device of universal consent. Without the contribution of the latter, the legitimacy of appropriating particular things remains unexplained.

From the standpoint of the interpretation of the argument, however, these substructures are independent. In other words, interpreting the first in terms of the apparatus of the consent problem does not entail that the second must be interpreted in terms of the maker's right doctrine, and vice versa. I shall begin with the argument for interpreting the first substructure in terms of the apparatus of the consent problem.

The apparatus of the consent problem comprises two elements: the generation of the consent problem from the original condition of the state of nature and its solution through the stipulation of the sufficiency condition. The consent problem is the problem of reconciling positive communism and the legitimate acquisition of individual property rights without recourse to the assumption of universal consent. Since Locke clearly affirms that everyone has a right to the earth in common (II, 25, lines

1–9), clearly acknowledges that this constitutes a prima facie difficulty for the legitimate acquistion of individual property (II, 25, lines 9–11), and clearly proposes to resolve this difficulty without recourse to the assumption of consent (II, 25, lines 18–21), the interpretative warrant for the first element of this apparatus is unimpeachable. It follows that it is a condition of adequacy on any interpretation of Locke's argument that it explain how Locke solves the consent problem.

For the purposes of reviewing the argument for my interpretation of Locke's solution to the consent problem, I shall assume that the stipulation of the sufficiency condition really does solve the problem and shall thus concentrate on the grounds for attributing this solution to Locke. There are three main grounds for doing so. The first is that this solution is congruent with and makes eminent sense of Locke's claim in II, 33–4 that appropriation which leaves enough and as good for others does not really take anything from the other commoners and does not injure them.

The second ground is that both steps of this solution's two-step identification of the natural right to property in common are required by Locke's texts. This is immediately apparent in the case of the first step—the identification of the natural right to property in common with the natural right to the means of preservation—because of Locke's explicit identification of these rights in the opening lines of chapter 5 (II, 25, lines 1–9). It is no less apparent, though rather less immediately so, in the case of the second step—the identification of the natural right to the means of preservation as the right (not to be excluded from the use of the common materials needed) to *produce* subsistence quantities of meat, drink, and whatnot.

The competing interpretation of this natural right identifies it as the right to *consume* subsistence quantities of meat, drink, and whatnot. The issue between these interpretations turns on the question of whether an able-bodied individual can exercise his right to the means of preservation other than by labouring. If he cannot, then our interpretation is upheld.

As alternative means of exercising this right, the competing interpretation proposes the rights of charity and inheritance. But since the former of these rights does not inhere in able-bodied individuals and the latter does not excuse them from labouring, they do not constitute alternatives in the required sense. We shall confine ourselves to the right of charity here. No able-bodied individual has a right to charity because a necessary condition of this right is that one have no means to subsist otherwise (I, 42). But all able-bodied individuals have the means to subsist otherwise, namely, their ability to labour. This conclusion is confirmed by one of Locke's letters to Molyneux, as well as by the analysis given in Locke's *Report to the Board of Trade*. Both of the proposed alternatives are further impugned by Locke's affirmation, in the *Two Treatises* and elsewhere, of the requirement that *everyone* labour for his subsistence, as far as he is able.

The third main ground for attributing this solution of the consent problem to Locke is that he explicitly argues, in II, 40–3, that labour's abundance guarantees that the empirical conditions required for the satisfaction of (what we have called) the second disjunct of (S) do in fact obtain.[1] He explicitly concludes from this that man 'had still in himself the great Foundation of Property' (II, 44)—still, that is, despite the advent of land scarcity. What is more, it is manifest from the marginal addition to II, 37 that Locke understood this argument from labour's abundance to be continuous with his claim that appropriation which leaves enough and as good for the other commoners does not injure them, that is, to be continuous with the operation of the sufficiency condition. Reading the argument in this way also allows us to respect the textual indications—in II, 40 and 44—that it forms an integral part of Locke's overall argument for the legitimacy of private property.

I turn now to the second substructure of Locke's overall argument, which I have interpreted in terms of the doctrine of maker's right. The argument for this interpretation is a complex one. Part of it—the negative part—rests on criticism of the traditional interpretation of this substructure. For the most part, however, the argument rests on two positive interpretative conclusions: first, that some of Locke's texts are individually best read in terms of the maker's right doctrine and, second, that the best sense of Locke's texts is to be made, on the whole, by reading all of them in these terms. I shall review these points in turn.

The negative part of the argument focuses, in particular, on criticising the traditional interpretation's derivation of the legitimating power of labour. In brief, the criticism is that not only is this derivation centrally

---

1. Recall that the sufficiency condition is satisfied whenever the second disjunct of (S) obtains.

Conclusion 147

founded on a fallacy, but also the premiss from which it begins is simply a special case of the conclusion it purports to establish. Since the proposed derivation is utterly vitiated by these flaws, I have concluded that hesitation in attributing it to Locke is therefore in order. I rejected the suggestion that the central flaw can be remedied by locating the traditional derivation in Locke's natural law framework, both because it failed actually to remedy the fallacy and because it required us to misunderstand the paradox of plenty.

Now the argument for the positive conclusion that some of Locke's texts are individually best read in terms of the maker's right doctrine is rather complex in its own right. The texts in question—I, 52–5 and the manuscript piece 'Morality'—are ones in which Locke adheres to the principle that the legitimacy of man's property in something derives from his having *made* it. In addition to establishing just this fact about these texts, the argument here also seeks to establish that there is specific interpretative warrant for the premisses on which this principle rests.

These premisses, it may be recalled, are as follows: (1) if one makes something ex nihilo, then one owns it; and (2) making and making ex nihilo are similar processes. Locke affirms (1) in a variety of places, including II, 6 and I, 53, but he does so most clearly and explicitly in the sixth essay of his *Essays on the Law of Nature*. Its status as a self-evident principle is confirmed by Locke's discussion in the *Essay* of a demonstrative science of morality (IV.iii.18, IV.xiii.3; cf. I.iv.13). The warrant for attributing (2) to Locke consists in the fact that the detailed respects in which I have elaborated the similarity there asserted are all drawn directly from the *Essay* (II.xxvi.2, III.vi.3, III.vi.40).

But the crucial element of this argument, of course, concerns the relevant texts themselves. I shall confine my attention to I, 52–5. I have argued that Locke's discussion of Filmer's argument that fathers have dominion over their children manifests his own adherence to the principle that a man's private property in something derives from his having made it. Locke manifests this adherence by accepting that the assumption that parents make their children entails the conclusion that parents have joint dominion over their children (I, 55), as this entailment holds only given the principle in question. I considered the objection that Locke is here merely assuming this principle *arguendo*, but dismissed it on the ground that it ignores the nesting arrangement of assumptions made *arguendo* that Locke adopts in I, 52–4. A further reason for reading Locke as adhering to the maker's right doctrine in I, 52–5 is that one is otherwise unable to account for the restriction of his concern there to a refutation of the claim that fathers *make* their children. For anyone who accepts the traditional derivation of labour's legitimating power, no such refutation can prove that fathers do not own their children, as Locke aims to prove.

It remains to recapitulate the argument for the positive conclusion that the best overall sense of Locke's texts is to be made by reading all of them in terms of the maker's right doctrine. This argument begins from the previous positive conclusion that some of Locke's texts are individually best read in these terms. It accepts that many other passages are more naturally read in the traditional manner, but holds that these passages *may* be read metaphorically in terms of the maker's right doctrine. Hence all of Locke's texts can be assimilated to the maker's right interpretation.

In this respect, however, the traditional and maker's right interpretations are asymmetrically related, for not all of Locke's texts can be assimilated to the traditional interpretation. Those texts that are individually best read in terms of the maker's right doctrine *cannot* be so assimilated, since the maker's right derivation of labour's legitimating power cannot be reduced to the traditional, labour mixture derivation. That is because the former derivation, but not the latter, is able to explain a man's property in his own labour.

It follows that the traditional interpretation of the second substructure of Locke's argument has to burden his texts with twin derivations of the legitimating power of labour. Since the best overall sense of this substructure and these texts is to be made by attributing to Locke but a single derivation of this power, the maker's right interpretation should thus be upheld.

The Limits of Lockean Logic

I have introduced the term 'Lockean property' to designate the determinate kind of private property right that actually follows from the logic of Locke's argument in the *Two Treatises*. I have argued that Lockean property is a use right that is subject to a multitude of specific limitations. Among these limitations, I have distinguished, somewhat artificially, between limitations in the nature of Lockean property and limitations that represent conditions on the legitimacy of Lockean property. Let us review each set in turn.

The limitations in the nature of Lockean property arise in virtue of the fact that the right to use a thing does not entail any of the other standard incidents of liberal ownership. Some of these other incidents (or elements thereof) represent what we have called permissible incidents of Lockean property: Lockean property is limited with respect to its permissible incidents in the sense that these incidents may be legitimately included in a more determinate specification of Lockean property only granted some supplementary argument or social agreement in favour of their inherence. I have argued that rights of transfer in cases of exchange belong to the permissible incidents of Lockean property. Some of the standard incidents (or elements thereof) represent what I have called impermissible incidents of Lockean property: I have argued that Lockean property may not legitimately include rights of transfer in the case of gifts, bequests, or the inheritance of surplus property.

The legitimacy of Lockean property, however specified in relation to its permissible incidents, is also subject to—and hence limited by—four conditions. Foremost among these is the sufficiency condition. I have argued that this condition requires the conservation of everyone's liberty of access to the means of production at the surplus level. The other three conditions on the legitimacy of Lockean property are the spoilage condition and the necessity of satisfying the disabled needy's right of charity and dependent children's right of maintenance (inheritance).

The advantage of distinguishing these sets of limitations is that the various limitations of Lockean property can then be more easily recognised as consequences of the logic of the Lockean theory of property. The limitations in the nature of Lockean property can be seen to obtain in consequence of the maker's right doctrine, and, if we ignore the limitations of Lockean property that are obviated by modernising the Lockean argument,[2] the remaining limitation on the legitimacy of Lockean property can be seen to obtain in consequence of the apparatus of

---

2. These limitations are the spoilage condition, the disabled needy's right of charity, and dependent children's right of maintenance (inheritance). Modernising the Lockean argument obviates these limitations because it eliminates the theistic premiss from which they derive in the *Two Treatises*, without replacing it with a functional equivalent.

the consent problem. The two sets of limitations can thus be seen, respectively, as consequences of the two substructures of the (modernised) Lockean argument.

The sense in which the first set of limitations obtain in consequence of the maker's right doctrine can be explicated as follows. I have accepted the plausibility of Locke's conclusion that (subject to the satisfaction of the sufficiency condition) the maker's right doctrine vests individuals with a use right in things they have made from unappropriated materials. For that matter, I have argued that the plausibility of this conclusion, such as it is, is in no way diminished by the adoption of a secular outlook, since the maker's right doctrine—even in Locke's theory—implies no commitment to theism.[3] Nevertheless, since the right to use a thing does not entail any of the other standard incidents of liberal ownership,[4] the Lockean argument does not establish on its own that any of these other incidents inhere in those on whom it has conferred ownership. The fact that the permissible incidents among these therefore inhere in Lockean owners only given some supplementary argument or social agreement— that is, the fact that Lockean property is limited with respect to its permissible incidents—may thus be seen as a consequence of the limited argumentative purchase of the maker's right doctrine on the standard incidents of liberal ownership.

This first set of limitations also includes, however, the limits of Lockean property that are imposed by its impermissible incidents. My discussion of this point was confined to a consideration of various rights of transfer. I argued that, in general, the possibility of what I called the potential owner's having a right of acquisition is a necessary condition of a right of transfer's being a permissible incident of Lockean property. I maintained that the inherence of a right of acquisition in a potential owner has to be justified independently of the legitimacy of a present owner's right of transfer.

Within a Lockean theory of property, the *only* justification that can

---

3. The doctrine implies no commitment to theism because to the extent that God appears, as it were, in its premisses, He appears only in the antecedents of conditionals.

4. This is established by the fact that the right to use can be held independently of the other standard incidents. Honoré recognises a wide interpretation of the right to use on which it comprises the right to manage and the right to the income.

be provided for the legitimacy of the potential owner's right of acquisition is the justification provided by her labouring, that is, by the maker's right doctrine.[5] In a Lockean property regime, then, a right of acquisition can be conferred on potential owners only if they can be construed as having laboured for it. I have argued that potential owners can be so construed in cases of exchange, but not in cases of unilateral transfer—gifts, bequests, and inheritance. It follows that in cases of gifts, bequests, and inheritance, potential owners can have no right of acquisition and hence that rights of transfer in these cases are impermissible incidents of Lockean property.[6] Thus, the fact that certain rights in property cannot be included in a more determinate specification of Lockean property may be seen as a consequence of the uniqueness of labour as the basis of acquisition in a Lockean theory.

Since the sufficiency condition itself belongs to the apparatus of the consent problem, the limitation it imposes on the legitimacy of Lockean property is straightforwardly explicable as a consequence of that apparatus. It is the satisfaction of the sufficiency condition that allows Lockean appropriators to forgo the consent of their fellow inhabitants of the state of nature. In the *Two Treatises*, the presumption that this consent is required is grounded in the supposition that appropriation violates everyone's right to property in common; in Nozick's theory, the presumption is grounded in the supposition that appropriation violates everyone's right to liberty (by restricting it adversely). To defeat this presumption and thereby to solve the consent problem, the Lockean theory of property holds that its underlying supposition is falsified when the sufficiency condition is satisfied.

I have argued that, in order to discharge the function thus assigned to it, the sufficiency condition must be interpreted so as to require the con-

---

5. Notice that modernising the Lockean argument makes this conclusion all the more evident. In our discussion of the argument of the *Two Treatises*, the uniqueness of labour as the title to property had to be established in face of the apparent alternatives provided by charity and inheritance. Since modernising the argument eliminates the basis of these rights altogether, there is no longer even the appearance of an alternative.

6. Inheritance *tout court* is an impermissible incident of modernised Lockean property, since the right of maintenance that previously vested dependent children with a right to acquire subsistence property from their parents' estate is eliminated by the modernisation of the Lockean argument.

servation of everyone's liberty of access to the means of production at the surplus level. Since everyone is originally entitled to this access in the state of nature, a weaker sufficiency condition would allow the institution of private property to injure some people by infringing their access to the means of production and would thereby reinstate the presumption that their consent is required. No attempt was made in general to determine the level of surplus production at which everyone's liberty of access to the means of production must be conserved, but a case was made that the sufficiency condition would, in any event, be satisfied by a regime of Lockean property that limited property in the material means of production to the greatest universalisable share.

The limitations of Lockean property that survive the modernisation of the Lockean argument, then, are those which issue from one or other of the substructures that define the logic of the argument itself. Since these substructures are characteristic of the Lockean argument for the legitimacy of private property, we may say that these limits inhere in Lockean property essentially. Since these same substructures are furthermore susceptible to modernisation, we may say that these limits also indicate the extent to which the Lockean argument is serviceable in defence of the legitimacy of the institution of private property.

Bibliography

Ashcraft, Richard. *Locke's Two Treatises of Government.* London: Allen and Unwin, 1987.
———. *Revolutionary Politics and Locke's Two Treatises of Government.* Princeton: Princeton University Press, 1986.
Baldwin, Thomas. 'Tully, Locke, and Land.' *The Locke Newsletter* 13 (1982): 21–33.
Buckle, Stephen. *Natural Law and the Theory of Property.* Oxford: Clarendon Press, 1991.
Cohen, G. A. *Marx and Locke on Land and Labour.* London: British Academy, 1985.
———. 'Nozick on Appropriation.' *New Left Review* 150 (1985): 89–107.
———. 'Self-Ownership, World-Ownership and Equality: Part II.' *Social Philosophy and Policy* 3, no. 2 (1986): 77–96.
Day, J. P. 'Locke on Property.' *Philosophical Quarterly* 16 (1966): 207–21.
Dunn, John. *The Political Thought of John Locke.* Cambridge: Cambridge University Press, 1969.
Dworkin, Ronald. 'What Is Equality? Part 2: Equality of Resources.' *Philosophy and Public Affairs* 10, no. 4 (1981): 283–345.
Fox Bourne, H. R. *The Life of John Locke*, vol. 2. London: Henry S. King, 1876.
Gibbard, Allan. 'Natural Property Rights.' *Noûs* 10 (1976): 77–86.
Held, Virginia. 'John Locke on Robert Nozick.' *Social Research* 43 (1976): 169–92.
Hohfeld, W. N. *Fundamental Legal Conceptions.* New Haven: Yale University Press, 1919.
Honoré, A. M. 'Ownership.' In *Making Law Bind.* Oxford: Clarendon Press, 1987: 161–92.
———. 'Property, Title, and Redistribution.' In *Making Law Bind.* Oxford: Clarendon Press, 1987: 215–26.
Hundert, E. J. 'The Making of *Homo Faber*: John Locke between Ideology and History.' *Journal of the History of Ideas* 33, no. 1 (1972): 3–22.

———. 'Market Society and Meaning in Locke's Political Philosophy.' *Journal of the History of Philosophy* 15, no. 1 (1977): 33–44.

Kirzner, Israel M. 'Entrepreneurship, Entitlement, and Economic Justice.' In J. Paul, ed., *Reading Nozick: Essays on Anarchy, State, and Utopia*. Oxford: Basil Blackwell, 1982: 383–411.

Laslett, Peter. 'Market Society and Political Theory.' *Historical Journal* 7, no. 1 (1964): 150–54.

Locke, John. *An Essay Concerning Human Understanding*. Edited by P. H. Nidditch. Oxford: Clarendon Press, 1975.

———. *Essays on the Law of Nature*. Edited and with an Introduction by W. von Leyden. Oxford: Clarendon Press, 1954.

———. *A Report to the Board of Trade to the Lord Justices 1697, Respecting Relief and Unemployment of the Poor*. In H. R. Fox Bourne, *The Life of John Locke*, vol. 2. London: Henry S. King, 1876: 377–91.

———. *Two Treatises of Government*, rev. ed. Edited and with an Introduction by Peter Laslett. Cambridge: Cambridge University Press, 1963.

Mack, Eric. 'Nozick on Unproductivity: The Unintended Consequences.' In J. Paul, ed., *Reading Nozick: Essays on Anarchy, State, and Utopia*. Oxford: Basil Blackwell, 1982: 169–90.

Macpherson, C. B. *Democratic Theory: Essays in Retrieval*. Oxford: Clarendon Press, 1973.

———. *The Political Theory of Possessive Individualism*. Oxford: Clarendon Press, 1962.

McKeon, Richard. 'The Development of the Concept of Private Property in Political Philosophy: A Study of the Background of the Constitution.' *Ethics* 48 (1937): 297–366.

Menger, Anton. *The Right to the Whole Produce of Labour*. Translated by M. E. Tanner. London: Macmillan, 1899.

Miller, David. 'Justice and Property.' *Ratio* 22, no. 1 (1980): 1–14.

Nozick, Robert. *Anarchy, State, and Utopia*. Oxford: Basil Blackwell, 1974.

Olivecrona, Karl. 'Locke's Theory of Appropriation.' *Philosophical Quarterly* 24, no. 96 (1974): 220–34.

O'Neill, Onora. 'Nozick's Entitlements.' In J. Paul, ed., *Reading Nozick: Essays on Anarchy, State, and Utopia*. Oxford: Basil Blackwell, 1982: 305–22.

Rashdall, Hastings. 'The Philosophical Theory of Property.' In C. Gore, ed., *Property: Its Duties and Rights*. London: Macmillan, 1913: 35–64.

Rogers, G. A. J. 'Locke, Law, and the Laws of Nature.' In R. Brandt, ed., *John Locke: Symposium Wolfenbüttel 1979*. Berlin: Walter de Gruyter, 1981: 146–62.

Ryan, Alan. 'Locke and the Dictatorship of the Bourgeoisie.' *Political Studies* 13, no. 2 (1965): 219–30.

———. *Property and Political Theory*. Oxford: Basil Blackwell, 1984.

Sargentich, Thomas. 'Locke and Ethical Theory: Two MS. Pieces.' *The Locke Newsletter* 5 (1974): 28–31.

Scanlon, Thomas. 'Nozick on Rights, Liberty, and Property.' In J. Paul, ed., *Reading Nozick: Essays on Anarchy, State, and Utopia*. Oxford: Basil Blackwell, 1982: 107–29.

Sen, Amartya. 'The Moral Standing of the Market.' *Social Philosophy and Policy* 2, no. 2 (1985): 1–19.

Shapiro, Ian. 'Resources, Capacities, and Ownership: The Workmanship Ideal and Distributive Justice.' *Political Theory* 19, no. 1 (1991): 47–72.

Simmons, A. John. *The Lockean Theory of Rights*. Princeton: Princeton University Press, 1992.

Snyder, David C. 'Locke on Natural Law and Property Rights.' *Canadian Journal of Philosophy* 16, no. 4 (1986): 723–50.

Steiner, Hillel. 'Liberty and Equality.' *Political Studies* 29, no. 4 (1981): 555–69.

———. 'The Natural Right to the Means of Production.' *Philosophical Quarterly* 27 (1977): 41–49.

Thiel, Udo. 'Locke's Concept of Person.' In R. Brandt, ed., *John Locke: Symposium Wolfenbüttel 1979*. Berlin: Walter de Gruyter, 1981: 181–92.

Tuck, Richard. *Natural Rights Theories: Their Origin and Development*. Cambridge: Cambridge University Press, 1979.

Tully, James. *A Discourse on Property: John Locke and His Adversaries*. Cambridge: Cambridge University Press, 1980.

Varian, H. R. 'Distributive Justice, Welfare Economics, and the Theory of Fairness.' *Philosophy and Public Affairs* 4, no. 3 (1975): 223–47.

Waldron, Jeremy. 'Enough and as Good Left for Others.' *Philosophical Quarterly* 29 (1979): 319–28.

———. 'Locke's Account of Inheritance and Bequest.' *Journal of the History of Philosophy* 19 (1981): 39–52.

———. 'The Turfs My Servant Has Cut.' *The Locke Newsletter* 13 (1982): 9–20.

———. 'Locke, Tully, and the Regulation of Property.' *Political Studies* 32 (1984): 98–106.

———. *The Right to Private Property*. Oxford: Clarendon Press, 1988.

Walzer, Michael. *Spheres of Justice: A Defense of Pluralism and Equality*. Oxford: Basil Blackwell, 1983.

Winfrey, J. C. 'Charity versus Justice in Locke's Theory of Property.' *Journal of the History of Ideas* 42, no. 3 (1981): 423–38.

Index

Able-bodied individuals, 44–46, 51, 103, 109, 116, 143, 145–46
Absence of term, 10, 99, 126
Abundance, age of, 35, 48, 90n, 143. *See also* Labour, abundance of
Access
  conservation of, 115–19, 138n, 139, 149, 151–52
  equality of, 113, 115–19, 136
  to materials, 5, 43, 54, 112–16, 143
  to means of production, 7, 135–39, 149, 151–52
  right of, 43, 51, 112–15
Acquisition, 21, 49, 107–11, 127, 140–41, 150–51. *See also* Appropriation
  original, 108–9
  principle of justice in, 122, 126n
  by transfer, 108–9
Agreement, social, 100, 107, 149–50
Alienate, power to, 10, 97
Animals, 85–88
Appropriation, 26, 47–48, 75, 111, 141. *See also* Acquisition
  completion of, 91–92
  labour's power to legitimate, 33, 59, 142
  under land scarcity, 54–57, 102, 115
  legitimacy of, 5, 28–29, 50, 55–59, 115, 141–42
  limited to use, 33–34
  opportunity to make an, 112–13, 123, 135
  of particular things, 59, 127–28, 142
  piecemeal, 117–18
  restrictions on, 37–40, 48–49
Aristotle, 21
Artificial things, 85–88
  defined, 64
Ashcraft, Richard, 13–18, 25, 42–43, 47, 69n, 72

Bargaining, 102
Baxter, Richard, 66n, 72–73
Bequests, 97, 104–7, 110, 126, 149, 151
Buckle, Stephen, 27, 28n

Capital, right to the, 10–11, 97, 101n, 106
Capitalist, 52, 117n
Charity, 41–42, 45, 53, 54n, 110
  as limitation of Lockean property, 102–5, 116n, 139, 144, 149
  as title to means of preservation, 41, 44, 145–46, 151n
Charles II, 16

Children. *See also* Inheritance; Maintenance
  as property, 77–84, 147–48
Civil law, 50, 91
Civil society, 18, 91–92, 100, 104, 117
Claim-right, defined, 113
Cohen, G. A., 57, 63n, 103n, 116n, 124n, 126–27, 133
Common, 16, 22, 24–32, 41, 43, 48–49, 51, 113–18, 121–22, 139–41, 144–45, 151
Communism, 48, 140–41, 143–44
Community of property, 24–27, 29
  negative, 24n, 26–27
  positive, 24n, 27–28, 30n
  redefinition of positive, 30–32
Compensation, 123, 130–32
Consent problem, 15–16, 18, 24–32, 75, 141, 144–45
  apparatus of, 5–7, 121, 144–45, 149–51
  constraint on solution of, 29
  defined, 25
  modernised, 122–23, 151
  solution to, 48–50, 59, 111, 115, 141, 145–46
  transposed as organisation problem, 117
Consequentialism, 131
Creation, 64, 69–76, 81–82, 125, 142. *See also* Making, ex nihilo
  defined, 63
  man as God's, 23, 73–74
  right of, 70–74, 81–82
Creationism, 70, 81–82
Cumberland, Richard, 22, 30, 71n, 73

Deontology, 131
Desert, 62
Digger, 16
Disability, 44–46, 53, 54n, 103–4

Distributive justice, 7, 121
Dominion, 23, 65, 70–73, 75, 77–81, 91, 142, 147
Dominium, 9n, 70–71, 77
Duration, 98–99, 126

Egalitarian, 4, 7
Employment
  duty of, 54, 101–2, 116n, 137
  right to, 54, 103, 111, 114, 137–38, 143
Enough and as good. *See* Sufficiency condition; Sufficiency limitation
Entitlement, 114–17, 139, 152
  different senses of, 113
  theory, 121–35
Equality, 16, 113, 115–19
Ethics. *See* Morality
Exchange, 106, 107n, 109–10, 149, 151
Exclusion crisis, 15
Exclusive right, defined, 30

Ferguson, Robert, 72
Filmer, Sir Robert, 13, 15, 24n, 25, 29, 77–79, 81–84, 141, 147
First taking, principle of, 127

Generation problem, 118–19
Gifts, 106–8, 110, 149, 151
Grotius, 6n, 16, 22, 24n, 25n, 26n, 66n, 127, 141

Hohfeld, W. N., 8n, 113
Homestead system, 101
Honoré, A. M., 9, 11n, 96–98, 150n

Idleness, critique of, 17, 43, 45–47
Incidents of ownership, 11–12, 96–100, 101n, 104, 106–7, 150
  defined, 9

permitted by Lockean argument, 107–11, 128–30, 134n, 149–51
standard enumeration of, 10
Inclusive right, defined, 30
Income, right to the, 10–11, 98, 150n
Inegalitarian, 4, 7
Inequality, 35, 136
Inheritance, 44–46, 97
  as limitation of Lockean property, 104–7, 110–11, 139, 144, 149, 151
  as title to means of preservation, 41, 44, 103, 145, 151n

James, Duke of York, 15

Labour
  abundance of, 54–57, 114, 117, 137, 143, 146
  finitude of, 35, 114
  full potential of, 114, 117, 136–37n
  as means of preservation, 41, 44–45, 53, 103, 146
  mixing, 33, 59–61, 83–84, 88–89, 148
  mixture metaphor, 18, 32, 62, 68, 88–89, 148
  obligation to, 44–47, 102, 116, 146
  property in one's, 33, 59, 61, 65–68, 89, 148
  theory of value, 55–57
  as title to property, 17–18, 32, 47, 109
  for wages, 51–54
Land
  equal division of, 117
  right to, 51–54, 114
Landless, 53, 54n, 101–2, 117n, 118
  complaints of, 111–15
Lapse of title, 101

Laslett, Peter, 22
Law of nature. *See* Natural law
Leveller, 16
Libertarianism, 122
Liberty, 135–39, 151
  defined, 113
  distinguished from licence, 33
  to produce subsistence, 114, 137
  to produce surplus, 7, 114, 137–39
  restrictions on, 122–23, 130–31, 139, 151
Lockean property
  conditions of, 113–17, 121, 135–39, 149, 151–52
  defined, 96
  egalitarian regime of, 7, 116–19, 152
  impermanence of, 118–19
  limited nature of, 106–11, 121, 130, 149–51
  modernised, 121, 128–30, 134n, 135–39, 149–52
  permissible incidents of, 107–11, 128–30, 134n, 149–51
Locke's property
  conditions of, 96, 100–106
  defined, 96
  indeterminacy of, 90–92, 100, 106–7
  nature of, 96–100

Mack, Eric, 131
Macpherson, C. B., 30, 52
Maintenance, children's right to, 46. *See also* Inheritance
  as limitation of Lockean property, 105, 110–11, 116n, 118, 139, 144, 149, 151n
Maker's right doctrine, 5–7, 18, 62–89, 98–99, 121, 125, 130, 137, 142, 144, 146–51
  assumed by Nozick, 124, 128

Maker's right doctrine (*continued*)
  contemporary plausibility of, 125
  defined, 62
  independence of God's existence, 63, 75n, 124–25, 150
  irreducibility of, 89, 148
  self-evidence of, 72–74, 76, 142, 147
Making
  analogy between God's and man's, 63, 75, 142–43
  in broad sense, 65–69, 74–76, 81, 84, 142–43
  criteria for, 83–85
  defined, 63–64
  ex aliquis, 142–43
  ex nihilo, 64, 74, 125, 142–43, 147. *See also* Creation
  intellectual dimension of, 65, 81
  process, 83–84
  in technical sense, 74–86, 125, 142–43, 147
Manage, right to, 10–11, 98, 150n
Market outcomes, 131
Masham, Lady, 45n
McKeon, Richard, 21
Means of preservation, 17–18, 41, 44–45, 103
  natural right to, 24, 41–47, 49–51, 53, 55, 102, 111–12, 140–41, 144–45
Methodology, interpretative, 13–15
Mixture. *See* Labour, mixing
Molyneux, William, 45n, 146
Money, 18, 31, 35–36, 38, 40, 143
Moral universe, changes in, 122
Morality, demonstrative science of, 69, 73–74, 76, 142, 147

Natural law, 28, 114, 115n
  analysis of property, 24, 140
  authority of, 23, 62n, 70–73, 140, 142
  bounds on property, 33, 39–40, 48, 100–101, 103–6, 143
  framework of Locke's argument, 6, 21, 34n, 40, 60, 120, 139–40
  fundamental, 22–23, 103, 140, 144
  pedigree of first taking, 127, 127n–128n
  second and third, 22n–23n
  tradition, 6n, 13, 22, 70–71, 140
Natural rights language, 16, 21, 122
Natural things, 85–88
Need, as basis of charity, 41, 45, 53, 103–4
Net worth, 132–33, 138
No-ownership, 122–123, 127, 130–31, 133–38
  arbitrary as baseline, 133–34
Nozick, Robert, 8, 34n, 36n, 60–61, 78, 83–85, 112–13, 120–38, 151

Olivecrona, Karl, 33n, 35, 57, 91n
O'Neill, O., 122n, 127
Ownership. *See also* Incidents of ownership
  common, 113–17, 121–22, 139
  full individual, 9, 96–99, 101n, 116n, 126, 128–29, 132–37, 138n. *See also* Private property
  less than full individual, 129, 134n
  split, 9

Paradox of plenty, 28–29, 30n, 49, 61, 147
Pareto-optimal, -superior, 129, 133–34, 138n
Person, 66–68, 76
  property in one's, 33, 59, 61, 65–68
Plato, 21
Poor law reforms, 42–43, 46

Index

Population growth, 118
Power relations, adverse, 115n, 117, 136
Preservation
  of mankind, 22, 29, 41, 103–4, 139–40, 143–44
  natural right to, 23, 41, 51, 104, 113–14
  of property, 90–92, 104
  of society, 22n
Private property. *See also* Lockean property; Locke's property; Property
  ambiguity of, 12
  concept of, 7–12, 128–29
  distinguished from property generally, 8
  legitimacy of specific rights of, 12, 95–100, 106–11, 128–30, 134n, 149–51
  liberal understanding of, 9–12. *See also* Ownership, full individual
  relation between general and specific notions of, 10–12
Productive bounty criterion, 133–35
  criticised, 135–39
  defined, 132
  generalised, 134
Productivity, 17, 54–57, 124, 129–30, 132–34, 143
Proletarian, 52
Property. *See also* Private property
  indeterminacy of, 8, 128–129n
  Locke's extended sense of, 53
  Locke's formal definition of, 32–33, 97, 109n
  right, 8–12
  and sovereignty, 70–71, 77, 142
  Tully's analysis of, 30–32
Proviso, 34–35, 40, 75, 82, 123, 141, 143. *See also* Spoilage limitation; Sufficiency condition; Sufficiency limitation
Pufendorf, 22, 127

Rashdall, Hastings, 3
Regress, Nozick's, 112–13, 123, 135
Rentiers, 117n
Right, different senses of, 8n, 113
Ryan, Alan, 61, 97n, 100

Sargentich, Thomas, 76
Scarcity, 40, 90
  age of, 35, 37, 143
  land, 18, 32, 35–37, 49–51, 54, 102, 111–15, 117–18, 146
  legitimacy of, 36–37, 50, 54
  local versus global, 118n
Selden, John, 22
Self-ownership, 33
Sergeant, John, 66
Servant/wage-labourer debate, 52–53
Shaftesbury, Earl of, 14, 17
Shapiro, Ian, 125n
Share
  equal, 116–17, 119n
  greatest universalisable, 117–19, 152
  right to one's, 30–32
Simmons, John, vii, 30n
Slavery, 53, 78
Sovereignty, 70–71, 77, 142
Spoilage limitation, 30, 34–35, 37–40, 48, 114n
  on Lockean property, 101, 139, 143, 149
Spontaneous products of nature, 85–88
State of nature, 16, 18, 25, 34–35, 90–92, 111, 116, 135, 139–41, 143–44, 151–52
  Nozick's, 122–23
Steiner, H., 116n, 117n, 118n, 119n

Suárez, 22
Subsistence, 45–46, 55–56, 104,
  110–11, 144, 146, 151n
  employment, 101n, 137–38, 143
  liberty to produce, 114, 137
  minimum share required for, 113,
   117n
  measure of, 114, 117n
  production, 5, 49, 59, 117, 141, 143
  right to consume, 24n, 41–42,
   44–45, 53, 103, 145
  right to produce, 43–44, 51,
   53–54, 114, 139, 145
Sufficiency condition, 49–51, 54–59,
  75, 82, 99, 101–3, 111–17,
  141–46, 149–52
  defined, 48
  modernised, 121, 123–24, 127,
   129–30, 132–39, 149–52
  taken seriously, 113–17, 135–39,
   149–52
Sufficiency limitation, 34, 36–37,
  39–40
Surplus, 7, 35, 57, 112–14, 137–39,
  149, 152
  inheritance of, 111, 149
  liability to charity, 44, 53, 104,
   110, 144
  redefined, 117n

Theological
  commitments, 4, 63, 75n, 122n,
   125, 150
  premisses, 6, 120, 125, 139, 149
Tories, 16, 25n

Transfer, 106–10, 126, 149–51
  principle of justice in, 126n
Transmissibility, 10, 99, 106, 117n–
  118n, 126
Transmission, 106–11
Tuck, Richard, 70, 71n, 77n
Tully, James, 30–32, 37, 42, 50–54,
  62–64, 66–67, 72, 81–82, 91n,
  97, 142
Tyrrell, J., 6n, 24n, 26–27

Universalisability, of property share,
  117–19
Use, 30–32, 107
  efficient, 118–19
  problem of, 21, 101, 126n
  right to, 10, 39, 97–101, 106,
   116n, 148–50

Value creation, 55–56, 62
Varian, H. R., 110n
Vazquez y Menchaca, Fernando, 77n

Waldron, Jeremy, 12, 26n, 27–28,
  37–40, 42, 47, 50, 53, 57,
  81–82, 84n, 97n, 104n
Welfare, economic conception of,
  132–33, 135
Whigs, 14–17, 25
Winfrey, J. C., 103n
Workmanship, 79
  man as God's, 22–23, 62n–63, 73
  model, 62–69, 71, 75–77, 81–90
Worsening the situation of others,
  122–23, 126, 130, 132–39